Dear
Amy,
Refuse to
Settle!
Blessings!.
Deaunde
10/30/06

You Don't Have To Settle!

Library of Congress Card Catalog No.: 2003098934
ISBN # 0-9747578-0-2

Cover Design: *Kelley*
Cover Concept: *Veraunda Jackson*
Page Design and Typography: *Kelley Melinn*
Author's Cover Photo and Headshot: *Rafael Tongol*
Author's Hairstylist and Make Up: *Elsie Knabb*

PRINTED IN THE UNITED STATES OF AMERICA
EHAP INC. NOVEMBER 2003

This book is available at quantity discounts for bulk purchases.
For additional information please contact
EHAP Inc. 407-445-1766 or email us at ehapinc@aol.com.

You Don't Have To Settle!

How to make your vision a reality!

Veraunda J. Jackson

Table Of Contents

Hello friends. I am Bill Yoast, one of the coaches portrayed in the Disney movie, "Remember the Titans." Since that movie, I have spoken on teamwork and leadership in almost every state in the country. Along the way, I have met many dynamic individuals, but at the top of my list is Veraunda Jackson. I had the privilege of hearing her speak at the National Consortium of Academics and Sports (NCAS) conference in Orlando, Florida in 2002. The response was incredible! I have never seen a speaker have such a profound effect on an audience. The same positive principals of personal enrichment which empowered her audience on that day, are clearly delineated in this book.

You know it is a funny thing when you look back on your life and try to figure out how and why things happened. I think we all would like to feel like we are special and believe we can make a difference. I am not one that looks back often, but as I sat on the front row listening to Veraunda ask, "WHY ARE YOU HERE?" so many things ran through my mind.

From my early childhood in Alabama as a poor kid born on a farm during the depression I tried to trace the events that brought me here today. At an early age I considered entering the ministry, but later realized the young people I wanted to work with weren't necessarily the ones who went to church. What better place than in the schools and on the athletic fields could I make a difference? You never know what life is preparing you for!

If it were not for a decision made by the Alexandria, Virginia school board in 1971, I would have never met Veraunda. Although she was only one years old, life was preparing to connect us many years later. The board decided the best way to achieve racial balance in the schools was to combine the three existing high schools into one, which became the T.C. Williams High School.

I had been in the school system for twelve years and was the head football coach at Hammond High School before this integration. Everyone, including me, thought I would get the head coaching job when the three schools were combined. As it turned out, the job was given to Herman Boone, Alexandria's only black coach who had been in the school system for only a year. I didn't understand why I had been hit in the face with a "NO." I was more than qualified for the job. I felt like my friends at the school board had turned on me. I felt the decision was unfair but decided to work with Herman as an assistant coach. Together we led the newly integrated T.C. Williams High school to the Virigina State Conference Championship and ended up being ranked the number two team in the country.

Initially, I experienced a range of emotions. Yes, I was angry, I was hurt, I was disappointed but sometimes not getting what you want can be a stroke of good luck. Thirty years later, Disney became interested in our story and told it in "Remember the Titans" starring Denzel Washington as Herman, and Will Patton as me.

I am here because the leaders of Alexandria did not settle! They did not take the easy way out; they did not do the most popular thing; they did not stay in the comfort zone. Instead they did the RIGHT thing. They placed the good of the community ahead of an individual. They created enemies. However, as Veraunda explains in this book, we all learned that you can be a bright light in a dark environment.

Now as Coach Boone and I speak to groups all over the country we are constantly reminded of Veraunda's words from her first book, "Everything Has A Price! The question is how much are you wiling to pay for it?" In her second book, Veraunda has once again made a resounding statement:

"You don't have to settle!"

I can assure you that wherever you are, whoever you are, whatever your dreams, every person and every situation you encounter can be the next step to making your dream a reality! I join Veraunda in wondering what YOU are being prepared for? YOU REALLY NEVER KNOW!

Acknowledgements

Faith without works is dead!

I would have lost heart, unless I had believed that I would see the goodness of the Lord in the land of the living. Wait on the Lord, be of good courage and He shall strengthen your heart!
Psalms 27:13-14

I am most grateful to my Creator for His constant grace and mercy. With Him, ALL things are possible! Thank you for constant favor! This journey has been a total leap of faith! The results have been awesome, and the best is yet to come!

I dedicate this book in honor of my mother, Vernita who always believed in the faithfulness and awesome power of our Creator. Thank you mother for the lessons that have made me the woman I am!

Thank you to my father, Herbert Sr. for showing me that hard work does pay off, but that there is always time for a smile and a word of encouragement. Daddy, your strength is amazing! To Mrs. Rose and my family I express my gratitude for your love, support and always believing in my possibilities! Grandma Vera, thank you for always calling in to let me know you are listening! I love each of you!!!

Thank you, Jaydee for always being there and enduring the "what-ifs?" with me. No matter what I dream, you support me 110%! I can never repay you for your unconditional support and belief in me.

To my sisters on the journey, Monica, Pam, Rosalyn, Ms. Paula, and Coach Trudi,...you have been a constant blessing! And still we rise! We are blessed indeed and our territories are enlarging!

A special thank you to my clients who put your faith in me. Each of you has taught me a valuable lesson. I am truly thankful for your constant support of my work!

Thank you to my webmaster, Brad, the entire downtown Orlando Kinko's staff...you really are my office away from the office. (Kelley, you are the best!) My gratitude to my accountant Al, and your staff for all of your hard work! There would be no EHAP, without each of you and your expertise!

No literary work is complete without the careful eyes of great editors. My appreciation goes out to Mrs. Miller, Shelley Parris, Sandra Smiley & Denise Jones! What an awesome team!

To all the readers, thank you for spreading the word...you are the best marketing tool in the industry!

Much love to all the writers and speakers I have met on this literary journey. Thank you for sharing your wisdom and giving your support! A special sisterhood hug and my sincere gratitude to Trevy for sharing so much of your publishing knowledge with me!

Finally, to my sorors: your support has been phenomenal! Thank you, ladies of Delta Sigma Theta Sorority Inc., for showing me true sisterhood and welcoming me across the country with open arms and hearts!

In memory of my mother, Vernita and brother, Herbert Jackson, Jr, (Herbie), I dream big, work hard, and know that I don't have to settle! I will fight the good fight and diligently work to empower those who have dreams and those who have lost hope on their journey!

TO GOD BE THE GLORY !!!

You Don't Have To Settle!

How to make your vision a reality!

The Opening Statement

Question: What would make a twenty-nine year old attorney at the peak of her career walk out of the legal profession and never look back?

Answer: The POSSIBILITY!

Let me explain. "You don't have to settle for anything!" And here is the kicker...you can have as much as you want! Prior, to November, 1999, all I ever wanted to do was be a lawyer. (Well, maybe have my own radio or television show.) I had both of those dreams come true before I was twenty-five years old. In college, I was a radio personality and a talk show host. At twenty-four I graduated from Law School. The next five years I had a very rewarding career as a prosecutor in Orlando, Florida. I loved my job!

When I tell people I was blessed, I mean it! I had a good salary, great benefits and moved up through the ranks quickly. So, why did I leave? One word: POSSIBILITY!

Don't laugh! Here is the truth: One day I was driving on the interstate when I had the scariest thought/vision. It was short, but powerful. I saw myself on a stage talking to thousands of people. I started freaking out! I had just begun to write my first book, *Everything Has A Price!* I didn't have three chapters written, didn't know how I was going to publish it, or how I would sell it, but in this vision I saw the book selling like hot cakes from the back of the auditorium as I was speaking.

1

I had a hundred questions. How was this going to happen? When was it going to happen? Whom would I employ? How would I make money? You get the picture. I was scared to death and overwhelmed by the POSSIBILITY.

Fear is powerful, but faith is awesome! For the next couple of days I played the "What if?" game. What if I don't sell a lot of books? What if I run out of money? What if I leave my job for this great vision and don't make it? (I never use the word fail!) About halfway through my "what ifs?", I asked myself the ultimate "what if?" question: "Veraunda, what if you are successful?" What do you have to lose? What if you get on Oprah? What if you travel the country and become famous? What if you make a million dollars? What if you can make money doing what you love, and make a difference in lives across this nation at the same time?

I had a good point, if I must say so myself. What if I made it? There was a POSSIBILITY...A GOOD POSSIBILITY!

How, when and where I made it was up to me. Did I believe enough in me to make the vision a reality? Lawyers think a whole lot, at times I believe we think too much. We are taught to look at all the options. The first rule of a good trial lawyer is try to find the weakness in your case, then look for your opponent's strengths. My analysis was short and sweet:

1. What do I have to lose? EVERYTHING!

2. What do I have to gain? EVERYTHING PLUS SOME!

That day, I knew my answer. After all, I had just finished writing half of a book challenging others to figure out what they were willing to pay for their success. Here was my opportunity to take it to another level. The POSSIBILITY of being an international motivational speaker and author could be a reality. But, I'd have to stop settling!

I would have to move out of my comfort zone. I would have to stop settling for the easy way out. I would have to stop giving up my dreams because they did not appear practical or realistic. I would have to change my thought process from contentment to desire. Sure, I had reached some of my goals, but I wanted more. Being a prosecutor for the government was great, but I could do and be so much more! Fear and anxiety kept me from getting it.

How many visions or thoughts have you had? What are YOUR possibilities? What if you make it a reality? What you have to lose should not be your focus, instead you should ask yourself what do you have to gain. The possibility is out there, but you have to stop settling for where you are! Life has so much to offer you. The only thing stopping you from making your dreams a reality, is you!

The challenge I present in this book is for you to stop dreaming and start living your dreams! Start figuring out what it would take to make your dreams come true. I bet you it isn't anything you don't have or can't get. So here is my formula for you:

Stop Settling! Dream Big! Work Hard! Then sit back and...enjoy the payoff!

Apply the lesson in this chapter to your life:

Describe in detail what your life would look like if you could do, have or be anything you wanted:

If you have ever had a dream or vision about your future, describe it here:

What scares you the most about pursuing this vision?

What do you have to loose?

"What If?"

Let me start by saying we could come up with a million what ifs! Both positive and negative. I know you have thought about what you would do *if* you won the lottery. I've thought about it a million times, one time for each dollar I would win. I have thought about what I would do with my tax refund *if* I get money back. The funny thing is, when I start coming up with what I am going to do with the money, I have no clue how much the refund will be. In fact, most of the time, I end up paying taxes, but each year I hold onto the thought, "What *if* I get some money back?"

One of the most common emotions I see when it comes to taking a risk, is fear. Trust me, I know what fear is because I have experienced it in many ways. I have experienced it in relationships, finances, career moves and my own personal insecurities.

I started teaching at a community college at the age of twenty-four. I taught public speaking for six years before starting my own business. Every single semester for six years, I feared the first day of class and the evaluations at the end of the semester. I would have butterflies in my stomach on the drive to campus. I would practice my opening night speech. "Good evening, I am Veraunda Jackson, and I have some good news and some bad news. The good news is we will get out a little early tonight, the bad news is we are going to give our first public presentation tonight." The students would look at me with the same look of surprise every semester. Is she really the instructor? How old is she? In turn I would share my professional background with them, hoping to let them know who was in control.

Then I would change my focus to assure them, this class was going to be both fun and challenging.

The catch was, I wanted them to like me. I wanted them to respect me. I was also afraid about what would happen if they didn't. It's very simple: I like to be in control. What ifs are a way for us to try to stay in control. We mentally run through all the scenarios to try to come up with a plan for every situation. Life never works the way we plan for it to work. In fact, life is so unpredictable it can't be controlled.

When you start a new adventure fear creeps in the same door that the excitement opened. The excitement rushes in with the new idea or relationship. It feels good. It sounds good. It looks good. BUT, as the days go by the fear creeps in. What if I don't make it? What if I can't make it? What if they hurt me? What if I can't pay my bills? What if people find out I made a mistake? Before you know it the fear of "what if" becomes consuming and stops us dead in our tracks. We trade the excitement in for safety. We start to believe where we are, is better than where we might end up *if* we fail in our new endeavor. So we never reach the possibilities simply because we are afraid of failure.

What if you decided deep in your spirit that FAILURE IS NOT AN OPTION? When I left the State Attorney's Office, I simply said a prayer asking for peace and wisdom. I knew I was going to need all the strength I could find to pursue my dream. But more importantly I knew my faith would have to sustain me as I started to navigate the unknown. There was one thing I knew deep down inside, I would not and could not fail! My faith said it in these words; "I have NEVER seen the righteous forsaken or His seed begging bread" (*Psalm 37:25*).

As an educator I learned very quickly I could not please everyone. In every class I have taught there are at least three people who think I could do something different. Some students complain about my strictness, others about the grading, and some just simply don't like me. I have been accused of having an ego problem. In five years of teaching speech I have had a few students appeal their grade. I have even had students who find my stories too graphic or offensive. During the beginning years of my teaching career I was easily offended. I took it personally. I wanted to please every student. I was definitely a firm instructor, but I also felt I was extremely fair. I tried to balance the course work with fun exercises. (Keeping in mind that public speaking is the most feared class in college.) I believed in providing positive feedback for every student on every speech. So when a student evaluation of my teaching had what I perceived as negative comments I would be upset. Couldn't the student see I was giving it my all? Couldn't they see I loved teaching? Couldn't they see I was always prepared? I typed my course outline. I graded papers timely. I even presented speeches to show them I wasn't asking them to do anything I couldn't do.

I would get so bogged down in the two or three negative evaluations that I ended up discounting the twenty or so positive evaluations. On some days, I felt like crying because someone had pointed out my weaknesses or imperfections as they saw them. If I live in my truth, I have plenty of weaknesses. If someone happens to verbalize or write his or her perception of me it gives me fuel to work on what I can and leave what I can't fix for another day.

Over the years, I have grown tremendously. I have been teaching now for almost eight years. I speak to thousands of people a year around the country. Thousands of people read my book each year. Thousands of people receive my "Thoughts that make a difference!" via electronic mail. There is no longer space in my world for what if people don't like me or what if people don't like what I have to say. The fact is, people won't always like me. People won't always like what I say and in many cases, they won't like how I say it. So "what if?" has to be dealt with accordingly.

I have refocused the "what if?" into a positive statement. I will never be able to please everybody, but "what if" I make a difference in thousands of lives while I am here on this earth? "What if?" that thousand takes my message to another thousand? The possibility of empowering millions of people with my message of hope, courage and perseverance becomes a reality *if* I just continue to do what I know to do with integrity, sincerity and passion.

Instead of focusing on all the negative "what ifs?" I have chosen to focus on the positive possibilities. I have chosen to focus on what I have confidence in. Some people perceive this confidence as arrogance. I see it as speaking my future into existence through my present state of mind. I see it as a form of controlling the negative thoughts and emotions by believing firmly in my abilities and my possibilities.

This may sound harsh, but other people are not a factor in my vision. Why? Because if I add their situations and their issues into my life I create more "What ifs?" that I have no control over. Think about this: What if my friends let me down? What if my husband/wife/mate doesn't support me? What if my co-workers don't do their jobs? What if my boss doesn't give me a good evaluation? What if my employees quit? What if my enemies plot against me? "What ifs" have a way of starting with one and multiplying very quickly. They have the ability to create a mountain of fear in a short period of time. The mountain of "what ifs?" becomes so huge that you start to question why you should try to climb it. The answer is you should climb...just because! Who knows what you will learn along the way.

The question shouldn't be what if people disappoint you because they will! The question should be who cares if other people don't act or provide what I want? I can guarantee that you won't always get the support you desire or need. I can promise you employees won't always do what you are paying them to do. (I know I have my days when my best is minimal.) I can assure you people will hate you and plot against you because they are cowards who are jealous of your courage. But as long as you keep climbing you determine your altitude, not the people around you or the situations you encounter on the way up. The question is how are you going to react when the "what ifs" happen? Will you let the "what ifs" keep you from your destination? Who knows what you will see and experience at the top? You climb, you toil, and you sweat because of the possibilities.

The last page of Oprah Winfrey's monthly magazine has an article written by her entitled, "What I know for sure." I love to read this article because Oprah always returns to the basics. I have learned there are numerous unknowns along our journey; they show up in our thought process as "What ifs?." They create fear, anxiety, and stress. To be successful, we must balance the "what ifs?" with what we know for sure.

What I know for sure is that I am a gifted speaker.
What I know for sure is I love speaking and would do it for free.
What I know for sure is each time I am speaking to five people or five hundred people for five dollars or five hundred dollars I am living my dream.

What I know for sure is that I can't please everyone. But I can make a difference in the life of one person at a time.

What I know for sure is I don't have to be perfect to make a difference.

What I know for sure is I have the opportunity to make a difference in millions of lives around the world.

What I know for sure is that the majority of people who hear me speak or read my book are blessed.

What I know for sure is that my heart is pure in my desire to inspire and empower people to live their dreams.

What I know for sure is life doesn't promise me a certain number of years on this earth, but it does promise me the possibility to live whatever years I have with peace and fulfillment.

What I know for sure is I don't have to settle.

What I know for sure is I have the power to create the life I want and by doing so, I create the ability to bless others in the process.

What I know for sure is I am excellent at what I do and I make a difference doing it!

In other words, what I know for sure is that my dream will become a reality simply because I choose not to settle for anything less!

Apply the lessons in this chapter to your life:

List all of the "what ifs?" you are experiencing as you think about pursuing your goals, dreams or vision:

List what you know for sure about who you are and what you are capable of doing:

What Are You Being Prepared For?

Some of my greatest truths have come while I was listening to someone else speak or reading a book. Something in the speech or on the page strikes me at full force and I say, "Wow, that's powerful!" The thought will keep coming back to me hours and days after I have heard or read it. Have you ever had something dwell in your spirit? Have you ever asked yourself what you were supposed to do with it? I'd like to suggest when your spirit is stirred, you are being prepared for something bigger and better. The stirring of your spirit by a thought, conversation or a book is the wake up call to get out of bed, leave your comfort zone and hit the ground running!

I am writing this chapter at the end of 2002. It is the end of December. I am sitting in a hotel room typing my heart away. Why is this important you ask? Most of this book has been written based on thoughts that have stirred my soul and spirit so much there was no question they were going to bless you as you read this book. I've been debating whether to include this chapter for a few months. The first time this title entered my mind, I wrote it in my little idea book then I left it. I woke up this morning before six. I have been taking one of my enjoyable soul trips. I traveled over to Tampa, Florida to spend the weekend just relaxing, reading, journaling and possibly writing. I have been reading three different books over the weekend. One was a novel, which I rarely get to enjoy, the second book was about relationships and the third book was about doing what matters in your life. When I woke up this morning I felt groggy, I jumped in the shower, then picked up the book on relationships.

I was reading and highlighting when I kept wondering "What are you being prepared for?" I was enjoying the book and finding it very enlightening. In essence the book was reaffirming the basis of any successful relationship is being honest with yourself and not allowing your fears to paralyze you. By the second chapter in the book, I was thinking, Sometimes there is too much work involved! Sometimes it easier to just be alone. I had to remember that everything in your life has a price! Yes, it is work, but the work is preparing you for something much greater than you can conceive. Then my mind flashed back to how I came up with the title of this chapter.

I attend a nondenominational church with over thirty nationalities. A few months ago, my church celebrated Hispanic heritage month. We had Latin music and dancers during our worship service. During the sermon we had a Spanish interpreter. At the conclusion of the service the members of the Hispanic community from the church served a wonderful array of Latin foods.

When the pastor started his sermon he told us it always takes him a few minutes to get adjusted to having an interpreter. The interpreter repeated what he said and the entire audience laughed. I didn't laugh for a very simple reason; I knew exactly how difficult it could be to speak to an audience while having someone repeat every word you said in a different language. I reflected on my days as a prosecutor when I had a court reporter typing every word I said and on many occasions simultaneously having a court interpreter speaking in a language I did not understand. I had to keep my thoughts fluent while addressing the jury. It was quite a task to balance!

While listening to my pastor and the interpreter, I realized by the time I was twenty-nine years old I had interpreters from almost every dialect in the world working with me on at least one case. I had become so comfortable with stenographers recording what I said and interpreters translating that I had to be in preparation for something! The something hit me while sitting in church. I was being prepared to speak to people all over the world! As I type this very sentence, I have chills along my spine and tears have formed in my eyes, because the greatness of this vision is overwhelming.

When you have a vision, there will always be a season of preparation. In most cases the preparation will involve different stages. Sometimes you will have lessons that take little effort to master. Other lessons will challenge the core of who you are. There are lessons you will have to comprehend prior to the next phase of your vision. When I started EHAP I had no idea how to run a company. I have had to spend a tremendous amount of time preparing myself for a position as the President and CEO of a major corporation. If you have a vision, I encourage you to take the initiative to learn as much as you can by reading, searching on the Internet, or speaking with people who are already doing what you want to do.

While you are in the season of preparation very rarely will you know what you are being prepared for down the road. Remember my original dream was to be a lawyer. I never wanted to be a motivational speaker or write a book. I never dreamed about traveling the world as a career. I was very happy as a prosecutor. I believed I was making a difference by fighting for justice. I felt like I had accomplished my goals and had made my family proud. Little did I know, being an attorney was preparing me for being an international speaker, trainer and author!

Once I embarked on my speaking career, I was quite comfortable traveling around the United States of America. I was excited about visiting new cities and states. But why settle for the USA when there is a whole world just waiting for us? On many occasions I was just happy to be getting paid to talk!

Your preparation usually starts very early. If I think about it, I have been in the preparation stage for over twenty years. It started when I was a little girl in the church plays. I was learning how to talk in front of people. My teachers would say I talked too much in class. It was true, I loved talking! I was being prepared for my future career. My mother would tell me to stop talking so much around the house. I was in preparation! It wasn't until I was in the seventh grade that a teacher saw my talking as a talent and directed me to the proper arena. She entered me into the local Optimist Oratorical contest. I placed second in that competition. The rest as they say is history!

I competed in speech and debate contests for five years straight. I won repeatedly. People would ask me why I talked so much? I would get an attitude, put my hand on my hip, then proceed to tell them, "I'll be talking my way to the bank one day!" Little did I know I was speaking my future into existence.

I headed off to Florida State University to major in talking. It is officially known as Communications. I was getting the formal preparation to go with my natural love for speaking. I was given the name Miss Oratorical within the first year of college. Any time a speaker was needed for an event, people called on me. My name was always popping up on someone's program as the speaker or commentator. I was being prepared! What other people hated to do, I loved! It made me popular on campus, but it also started providing opportunity after opportunity. My mouth was creating a wonderful path for me.

One day I was running my mouth while standing in a line to purchase books for my junior year at Florida State University. A local radio station was broadcasting live for the first week of school. The on-air personality was a man by the name of Eric Angel. He must have seen me just talking up a storm. He walked over with his microphone and I instantly decided I did not want to be on the radio! I was in college to be the next famous talk show host or television news anchor, not a radio personality. To be honest, I thought being on television was much more prestigious than talking on the radio. Eric kept asking me questions while I kept trying to get him to go away. Finally, he told me I had a beautiful voice that should be on the radio. I auditioned for a job with the station a week later. For the next two and a half years I would be the sexy and seductive on-air personality, "Cindy Spice!"

See what I mean? Your gift will create opportunities for you even when you don't see them coming! At nineteen years old I had a job that half of the students in the College of Communication would have killed for. Now, take this one step further, I was meeting every music entertainer who came to town. I had an opportunity to socialize with them. I was being prepared! I saw all kinds of things that left a lasting impression on me.

Most of the artists were down to earth and approachable. I found myself watching how they interacted with their fans. Many of the biggest names in the business at the time were extremely nice. To name a few, I loved Boyz II Men, En Vogue, Billy Idol, Lou Rawls, New Edition, and Patti Labelle. On the other hand, I had also seen entertainers do cocaine, smoke marijuana and perform while intoxicated. Most of these entertainers were a royal pain to interact with. At a very early age I was being shown what life in the limelight could be like. I was also being shown each person has a choice in the process.

I often wondered if people realized that not being prepared could be devastating to your career. Too much too fast is a deadly combination. We have seen it time and time again. A young entertainer or athlete makes it to the big leagues then does something to lose it all or mismanages their finances. We always wonder how they could waste millions of dollars or why would they use drugs? I have known the answer since I was a radio personality. The money and the fame doesn't fulfill them. It is a great dream they have imagined all of their lives. Yes, they've been singing or dancing all of their lives. But they weren't prepared for the costs of the profession. All they saw on television was the glamour. If they had taken the time to research the profession they would know "Everything Has A Price!"

Let me give you another example. Now that I am traveling the country I have realized traveling for work is very different than traveling for vacation. If you don't find a way to balance sitting in airports for hours, sleeping in strange beds, being disconnected from friends and family, you could end up being depressed or resenting the job. As a motivational speaker and author, the last thing I need is to be out of balance before a presentation. So I have watched other people who travel for a living. I always have a good book and a magazine. I have started lodging in chain hotels to provide some familiarity. I make it a point to talk to friends daily via cell phone to stay connected. This is all a part of the preparation. If you are not grounded, the sparkle of the vision will wear off very quickly. You will begin to focus on all of the challenges instead of figuring out a way to make the process work for you. The process is vital to the vision being successful!

What are you being prepared for? Think about what you love to do. Every career counselor, life coach and motivational speaker will tell you to find something you love so much you would do it for free, that is where your wealth will come from. I can tell you from personal experience if you are passionate about your work, your passion will produce your purpose.

I have no doubt in my mind; my mission is to use my ability to speak to make a difference in lives around the world. How do I know? It's simple, my entire life, I have been using my ability to speak. Life has been preparing me since I was a little girl to get on platforms to motivate and empower people to live their dreams!

When you look at your life, what is it that you have been doing which comes naturally? What is it that you do better than anyone else? Perhaps, you can't immediately identify it. Don't worry, with time your purpose will become clear. But you have to give it some serious thought and be willing to be patient as the process prepares you.

I was talking to my hair stylist one day while she was styling my hair. She has a beautiful salon and I asked her what made her want to be a hairstylist. Her response was, "I have loved styling hair since I was a little girl." Her mother had been a hairstylist. She loved the environment in the salon. She has owned her salon for over twenty years. She has a very successful business along with a loyal clientele. She is very professional and very dedicated.

When I speak to young people about their dreams I include my hairstylist's story because you can be successful doing anything! Don't settle in your life based on how other people define success. You don't have to be a lawyer or doctor to be successful. It is not about how many college degrees you have or how much money you make. I believe education is important, I also believe in being comfortable. But some of the most powerful and successful people are the people you don't read about everyday. They are our teachers, police officers, firefighters, correction officers, plumbers, lawn specialists, electricians, executive assistants, telephone operators, and truck drivers. They are people who love their jobs and make a difference in the lives of others every day.

Our society is a cruel one! From childhood the adults in our lives define success for us. Little boys shouldn't do hair. Little girls shouldn't play with fire trucks. We are told what professions are successful and which ones are not. People make us feel inadequate. Based on what they say about us or believe about us we start to settle. We have to go back to our truths! From the day we are born we are being prepared for something.

Little boys and girls play cops and robbers. They are being prepared. Little boys and girls play with fire engines. They are being prepared. Little girls and boys play with chalkboards as if they were teaching school. They are being prepared. Little girls and boys enjoy doing other people's hair. They are being prepared. Little girls and boys enjoy taking things apart and putting them back together. They are being prepared. Little girls and boys enjoy reading about science or animals. They are being prepared.

What about you? What have you been prepared for? What do you enjoy? How can you merge your skills into a fulfilling career? If you are already doing what you love, then the next question is how can you take it to the next level? How can you make it better? Can you find a way to enjoy what you do even more? Can you create more freedom for yourself and your family?

We need you to do what you love! We need you to be so good at it that people will pay you to do it! We need you to be prepared when the opportunity comes! We need you to refuse to settle! When you live your dream, we all become beneficiaries. You do a great job, because you are doing what you have been prepared to do! You can withstand the challenges, because you are doing what you were meant to do! When you are living according to your purpose, the obstacles become opportunities. I challenge you to focus your energy on your purpose. While you are searching for the answers remember, in the meantime you are being prepared for something great! You may not be able to put all the pieces together at this moment, but just hold on. The answer will appear when you least expect it! The people and the resources will appear when you need them. Just be prepared to enjoy the journey! You never know what life has in store for you. Pay attention to the signs that will lead you to your divine purpose. What are *YOU* being prepared for?

Apply the lessons in this chapter to your life:

What is the one thing you love doing?

What do other people compliment you on?

What professions utilize your talents?

What do you need to do to put your talent into a form so people will pay you for it?

Who Cares?

Don't you get tired of people telling you what you can and can't do? My favorite scenario is people asking me *how* I am going to do something. In most situations they really don't care how it is going to get done. What they are really saying is your vision seems a little too big for someone like you. When I started writing my first book, I only told close friends about the project. As the book was about to be released, I started spreading the word I had written a motivational book. I also announced I was going to take a leap of faith and pursue a speaking career. Would you believe people told me I should reconsider leaving my job? People asked me how I was going to pay for the book to be printed. Some folks were bold enough to ask me how much it cost me to print the books and how much money I was going to make. The question in my mind was always, "Do you *really* care?" You know and I know, the answer was no, they didn't care! They were just being nosey. I now know many of them were hoping I would fail. How sad!

People can get us in a lot of mess! The troubling thing is when the rubber meets the road, they will be nowhere in sight. In fact, they will be the people who cause you pain, keep you trapped in a dead end job, or a bad relationship. Your friends will tell you to leave, when you should stay or to stay when you should leave. One of the most frustrating lines I have heard during my life is, "If I were you..." There have been times when I want to scream..., "well you are not me!" A week later I find myself trying to help someone cope with a problem and using the same terms. People don't want our negativity; they want our unconditional support and love.

We care so much about what others think. We want to fit in with the norm or status quo. According to most studies, one of the biggest fears we have is the fear of being rejected. So we find ways to belong. Belonging to the wrong group, can get you killed!

While I was assigned to the felony prosecution division as an Assistant State Attorney, I received a challenging case that proves in the long run, who you associate with can make a tremendous difference in where you end up.

The case was a high publicity case. I have changed the names to protect the identity of those involved. It started out as a simple argument. A teenager's bike had been stolen. When he saw a young man with his bike the teenager confronted him. Things quickly went down hill. Once the teenager accused the other of stealing his bike, heated words were exchanged. Both parties went their separate ways angry and vowing revenge. I will name the teenager, Trevor and the young man, Jose.

Trevor was in school and working a part-time job. Jose on the other hand was close to eighteen and a member of a violent street gang. When Trevor accused Jose of stealing, Jose became outraged and exclaimed, "My gang doesn't steal!" It always amazed me that there is honor in gangs. This gang actually had a bible, (this is what they called their rules and laws) which listed stealing as a dishonorable crime. Now this would have been a sign for me to leave him and the bike alone. Instead, Trevor approached an adult friend who lived in the apartments and pleaded for his help. The adult, Pablo, listened to the story and didn't take a big interest in the situation until Jose rode by on the bike as they were walking to the corner store. Pablo decided to ask for the bike to be returned. Jose's response was one of total disrespect. He made it clear, he didn't care! He didn't care that Pablo was an adult. He didn't care about how Trevor was going to get to school and didn't care about the police getting a theft report.

Pablo, who admittedly had a beer or two, was upset that Jose was disrespecting him and fired back some not so pleasant words. Remember the moral of this chapter is who cares? Jose didn't care! In fact, what seemed like a trivial matter quickly became one of life and death. Within an hour or so Jose had changed Pablo's life forever!

While Trevor and Pablo walked back to the apartments, Jose rode to a nearby apartment complex to enlist the help of some soldiers. Soldiers in gangs are the enforcers. They are the ones who take care of problems and do the dirty work. There is an organizational system in these gangs that would give the local police department a run for their money. There is a hierarchy of leadership, there is a protocol of how to handle disputes, and there is a process of taking care of business.

The first step Jose had to take was contacting the Vice President of the gang to advise him of the problem. This is the same as a briefing in corporate America. First he met with Sergio and gave him a brief version of his confrontation with Trevor and Pablo. He was instructed to go get the soldiers. To do this Jose contacted the Vice President's girl friend, Rita. Rita was the secretary of the gang. She kept records on all the members, including applications with pictures, disciplinary actions and current contact numbers. She was also the mother of two children and expecting a third child. When Jose told her what had taken place, she immediately started calling the soldiers.

When I read the reports, I was amazed by how quickly the soldiers were willing to get involved in the battle. A battle that would cost them dearly. There were no questions asked. Based on the word of one member, life would change for countless people. Two of the soldiers responded to the apartment immediately. Sergio was one of the Vice Presidents of the gang. Based on his criminal record, he had earned his position fair and square. He had just returned from Miami, Florida doing a drive by shooting in a stolen car. Sergio was in his mid to late twenties. But the hardness of his lifestyle showed on his face. He had numerous tattoos depicting various signs of the gang life.

The other soldier was in his late twenties also. He was the father of a young child with a second one on the way. He was married and had a respectable day job. His nickname was Muerte. As the tattoo on his right arm illustrated, the name stood for the angel of death. When he got the call from Rita, he was just getting in from work. I'm sure he thought it was just going to be a quick meeting, perhaps a fight, if he was lucky he could get back home in time for dinner with his wife and his young daughter. Gang members do not discuss business on the phone. So he didn't find out what the assignment was until he arrived.

How many times have you rushed to someone's rescue with no idea of what you were getting yourself into? How many times have other people only told you half of the story? When you arrived you realized the problem was a disaster waiting to happen and you really should have stayed clear of the mess. But by then, it's too late; you've been pulled into the situation and don't know how to get out.

Gangs function extremely well, because they *accept* people for who and what they are. They don't care about your weaknesses or past record. As long as you will be loyal to the gang and its mission, you will always be supported and accepted. This particular gang had some interesting programs. They raised funds for families of members who were imprisoned. They tolerated no disrespect of the women involved with gang members. What more could an individual ask for? Not only would they take care of the gang member, the gang would take care of their family. When you are not clear on who you are and what you stand for, it is easy to find yourself wanting to belong. Often belonging will cost you, because the reality of life is, NO ONE will take better care of you than YOU! The three gang members would learn this lesson the hard way.

When the three soldiers met, Jose recounted the story of the confrontation. There was only one option, teach Trevor and Pablo a lesson. The next question was solved quickly. How are we going to enforce the lesson? Rita was the clerk of the property. She was asked for the weapons. Her boyfriend had two weapons at the house. A pistol and a shotgun were kept in the bedroom closet for emergencies just like this one. Choosing which weapon was simple. The pistol was registered so the soldiers would have to use the shotgun. The shotgun is a powerful weapon, instead of shooting one single bullet; it sprays hundreds of pellets smaller than bb's. The spray of the pellets increases your chance of hitting the target. The damage the pellets can do to a human body is unbelievable. They can literally blow you apart.

With the shotgun in a box, the soldiers took their place for battle. Muerte drove the stolen car. It was a dark colored, four door compact car. Jose sat in the front passenger seat; his role was to point out Trevor and Pablo. Sergio sat alone in the back seat. The ride was a fairly short one. There was just enough time and distance for Sergio to assemble the shotgun and load it with shells. There was no discussion about what to do or how to do it. What happened next is chilling!

The car circled the apartment complex where Trevor and Pablo lived about five times. The soldiers inside had an unnerving sense of calm. Jose saw Trevor and Pablo standing on a second story balcony. He stated matter of factly, "That's them." The sun was setting and there was just enough light for Sergio to get a good look at his target. According to witnesses, the back window rolled down and there was a loud shot. Pablo didn't even see it coming. Trevor did, but it was too late. There was only one shot. The shot was the work of a polished marksman. Pablo had been shot in the upper torso area. His body slumped to the ground. Blood was spattered everywhere. Everyone panicked and a climate of disbelief arrived with the sunset! People, who were nearby screamed, others who heard the shot, dialed 911. Trevor couldn't believe he had not been hit. What did hit him was the grim reality that the shot was probably meant for both of them. Trevor was lucky to be alive and Pablo was going to have to fight for his life. He was rushed to the trauma unit at a local hospital.

The soldiers sped off in the car. No one got a tag number, the windows were tinted and witnesses didn't want to get involved. During the drive after the shot had been fired, Sergio was calmly advising Jose, to slow down, so he would not draw attention to the car. There was a nervous energy now between Muerte and Jose. Muerte was told to drive to Sergio's girlfriend's apartment, a few miles away. Once they arrived at the apartment the soldiers took the shotgun inside, and tried to remain calm. Sergio gave quick orders to his girlfriend and the soldiers. While she got them different shirts, they shaved and decided to split up.

How many times have you allowed people to manipulate your behavior? Then when the situation turned ugly, you were shocked they did not care about you? Were you surprised when they tried to save themselves? As a prosecutor, the one thing I can tell you, is when everybody is in trouble, everybody will look out for himself or herself, it is human nature. They will always choose to save themselves before you. I can't recall one case involving more than one defendant when at least one person didn't hang the others out to dry to reduce his sentence.

The scenario is always the same. People make an issue or idea sound bigger than it really is. We get all excited and hyped about it. No questions are asked and even if they are, the ringleader dismisses them as trivial issues. They make statements like don't worry about that, or we will deal with it when it comes up. That is exactly the problem! When it comes up, everyone is dealing with their own issues. Who cares about you when they are about to lose everything they have?

I can recall crying on an associate's shoulder one day about a problem. To be fair, it was an ongoing problem and I had not been able to come up with a clear-cut answer. Waiting on an answer was killing me! When I rehashed the issue with this associate for the thirtieth time, she hurt my feelings. I remarked about how tired I was of the situation and she didn't miss a beat. "I know, you are tired because I'm sick of hearing about it!" I was crushed. In other words, who cares? Answer? "I don't!" This was someone who had lived in my home during a crisis, someone I had listened to cry when she was in pain, someone who would ask to borrow money when she was broke. But now, when I was in need, who cared?

Did she intentionally not care about me? Probably not, nevertheless, it hurt. It made me very aware of how careful we have to be about letting people in our world and trusting them with our fragile information. When I think back, this same friend had remarked on how long it took to get to know me, how guarded I was, and how anti-social I could be. Well, in light of the outcome, perhaps, I should have been a bit more careful. Or as the editor of this chapter pointed out, not told the same story over and over. But as humans we tend to repeat ourselves.

The good news is when people show me who they are I believe them. I am a quick learner. Once I process the information, and realize you do not care about me or what is in my best interest, I let you go. There is no purpose in keeping people in your life who show you they will turn on you. In the gang culture, traitors are severely punished. Many times the consequence is death! Why? It is simple; lives are depending on the loyalty of the gang. As a member of the gang, you depend on each member to have your back when there is a confrontation with the enemy. Loyalty is not optional it is required! You don't expect fellow members to run or snitch. Gangs operate on secrecy and trust. They accept people who have been rejected or abandoned by others. They make a pact to take care of, support and protect each other. And yes, even die for each other if the situation calls for it. So why didn't those vows of loyalty work in this case? The answer is simple, when it is you or me, most people will choose themselves first! It's called survival.

My trial partner at the time was a young man who I have the utmost respect for, John Pare'. I always describe him as a handsome FBI looking young man. John and I had been friends for a couple of years. He arrived at the State Attorney's office shortly after I did. He was a smart and diligent attorney. When I was assigned the case, I knew I was going to need help. John was my first choice. I asked, (really I begged) my supervisor to assign him as co-counsel on the case. I was good, but five defendants with five attorneys was not a match up I wanted to tackle alone. John and I had a total of seven years experience. The defense attorneys had well over an estimated seventy years of experience amongst them. John and I had quite a case on our hands. The one thing in our favor was my experience with gangs in the juvenile unit and John's growing up in Chicago. Prosecuting gangs is like prosecuting sex crimes; most defense attorneys only have specialized cases like this once in a blue moon. I on the other hand, had tried several gang cases. What the defense attorneys take for granted is if you are young, you are also naive. John and I both had been exposed to the street in public schools. My exposure came in Orlando, his, by way of growing up in Chicago. Together, we would make an awesome team. Our youth would definitely work in our favor.

After talking to the Orange County Sheriff's Office gang unit and looking through the box of reports, we started taking depositions. This is a process of having witnesses come in and asking them a series of questions in the presence of all the attorneys to evaluate the case and determine the credibility of the witnesses. The witness list in this case was long. There were over thirty witnesses including law enforcement officers. John and I divided the list. Unfortunately, many of the witnesses didn't want to get involved.

Forcing us to ask the question again, who really cares? Here is a situation where someone's life is hanging in the balance and people don't want to get involved for fear of retaliation. This proves my basic theory to be correct about people watching out for themselves.

Many people said they only heard the shot, but did not see anything. Others could describe small details like a dark compact car or the shot came from the back passenger window. Sometimes the wheels of justice turn very slowly. In this case, John and I were fighting an uphill battle. We received a big break when we learned Jose's girlfriend was at the apartment's pool and saw the car circling. She was sure Jose was on the passenger side and Muerte was the driver. Jose's sister was also at the pool and saw her brother and Muerte in the car. Our challenge was to get them to take the witness stand.

While writing this chapter, I called John to ask him what stuck out in his mind the most about the case. John doesn't show emotions very often, so I was very interested in his reflections. I didn't tell him what my take on the case was. I wanted his true thoughts; after all, it had been over three years since we prosecuted the case. Whatever stuck out in his mind would have to be relevant. In fact, what stood out in his mind was almost profound given the title of this chapter, which I had not shared with him prior to asking him for his input.

John remembered covering a deposition with all five of the defense attorneys present. Several witnesses had come in and testified they did not see anything. At the conclusion of the depositions, the defense attorneys started asking John how could we prosecute this case? We had no evidence against their clients. Nobody saw who did it. There was no way we could win this case! Knowing John as I do, I know he was calm and collected. He was probably leaning back in his chair exhibiting a non-chalant attitude as the defense attorneys began to celebrate their victory.

John told me as they began gloating about what we couldn't do, they had forgotten about why we were prosecuting this case. It was our duty and responsibility to seek justice on behalf of a victim who was fighting for his life. But they could care less about our victim. They were concerned about their clients and how this prosecution would affect them. In their minds, they had already won the case. But as John said so confidently to me when he returned from the deposition, "They shouldn't pat themselves on the back too soon!" I agreed with John, never underestimate the underdog! They will fight with everything they have. We had nothing to lose by trying this case and we were going to fight for Pablo with everything we had!

When we were first assigned the case, the victim was still in the intensive care unit at the hospital. John and I went to see the victim a few months into the case. It is a miracle he lived. It took months for him to be released from the hospital. The final diagnosis was sad. He would be paralyzed from the chest down for the rest of his life. John and I were accompanied by a gang agent to Pablo's home for an interview. I was legally prepared. I had a list of questions ready for him. I had tried all kinds of cases including other gang cases. I knew what I was doing. I had seen a lot in three years with the State Attorney's office. Whenever you think you have seen it all, get ready, there is always something else that can shock you.

We traveled to a small three-bedroom apartment on the southwest side of Orlando. Pablo's mother met us at the door. The sadness in her eyes was the first indicator this was not going to be an easy task. His father greeted us next with a firm handshake. His eyes were filled with a solemn look of pain. Pablo had only been home a couple of weeks. Reality was taking a toll on the whole family. Pablo would never be able to walk again.

At twenty-six years old, I could not imagine what being paralyzed felt like, but when I walked into Pablo's bedroom, my heart sank. It was a tiny bedroom. Pablo lay perfectly still in a special medical bed. He looked over at me and I wanted to cry. Agent Rivera, introduced himself first, I was next and then John. I tried to focus on my reason for being here. But I found myself just staring at Pablo. His arms lay limp at his side. He had regained a little feeling in his upper body. From time to time his hands would make small uncontrollable movements.

I asked Pablo how he was doing. What a dumb question! He was paralyzed. Life for him had become a living hell. After I asked, I couldn't take it back. With tears in his eyes, he said his loss was devastating. His whole life had been changed because he tried to help a young man get his bike back. His girlfriend couldn't deal with the injury and she had abandoned him. He had a two-year-old daughter he could no longer lift or play with. His voiced was filled with anger and disbelief. John and I sat perfectly quiet listening intently. There was nothing we could say to console Pablo. As he finished, he looked at us and said he couldn't do anything for himself. With a tone that pierced my heart he asked did I know what it felt like not to be able to feed yourself, shave, brush your teeth or go to the bathroom by yourself. The truth was, no I didn't know what it was like. I couldn't even imagine it!

I managed to get through the list of questions I had for Pablo without breaking down in tears. Once we started talking about the facts, the conversation moved a little quicker. Pablo didn't remember a lot about the actual shooting, but he did remember the confrontation and the events leading up to the shot. His delivery was very choppy. The details were not enough to convict anyone. He saw the car circling, but thought nothing of it at the time. The windows were tinted so he couldn't see anyone in the car. When the car came around for the second time, he heard the shot, but never saw a gun. His body went limp and he realized he had been shot.

Of the five defendants, the only one who did not cooperate at some point was the vice president of the gang. He was true to the end. But the real question is "Who Cares?" The soldiers were all charged with attempted first-degree murder. Jose and Muerte were found shortly after the shooting thanks to the information from Jose's sister and girlfriend. The judge set their bonds high, because both were a flight risk. The Orange County Sheriff's office obtained an arrest and search warrant for Sergio. They caught him off guard at his house. With all three of the soldiers in custody, the women were next.

Sergio's girlfriend was picked up on a warrant at her home. The shotgun was found in the bedroom closet under a pile of clothes. In the pile was a bright yellow basketball jersey Jose had been wearing when Trevor and Pablo saw him at the store. We caught Rita just in the nick of time; she was leaving her apartment loading a suitcase full of gang records into her car. The records were impeccable. There were files on each member of the gang. The file included a photo attached to their application. Yes, you read it right! You have to fill out an application before you can become a member of street gangs!

The application is quite amusing. It asks you for the basic biographical information: name, date of birth, address and phone numbers. But because this was a Latin gang, you had to confirm you were a member of the Latin race. The application also had a section for criminal history just like employment applications. The part that caught my attention was the inquiries into the facts surrounding the case, and whether the member had to serve time for the charge. Members were bold enough to list their charges, (most were drug offenses) and then mock the justice system by writing comments like "got off" or "beat the case."

There was another question that struck me as a joke. It basically asked whether or not the applicant understood the gang was an association that was law abiding and served to fight injustice in the prison system. Each member had to circle yes, indicating they understood. Yeah, right! Each of the three soldiers had an application complete with photo in the suitcase. Amazing!

As if the applications were not enough, there were also discipline reports in the suitcase. Now this is where I said, you have got to be kidding me! Send kids to school and they fail English, writing and math classes. But put them in a gang and they can keep records better than secretaries in corporate offices can! These kids are intelligent and with the right or wrong environment, they are groomed for success. Success of course is relative. This gang had a history of success. Success selling drugs, success dealing in stolen property, and success in avoiding arrests. They were successful criminals.

The discipline reports were incredible. They were typed forms, just like the applications. There was a line for the member's name, the date of the infraction and a detailed description of the offense. The member had an opportunity to respond (in writing) to the allegations. Once the paperwork was complete, the discipline report was reviewed by an officer and in some cases a hearing was held. The final line of the form recorded the final disposition and what form of discipline was imposed.

I was not surprised to find out Sergio had been reprimanded a couple of times. His latest infraction was recorded as failure to kill the victim in the drive-by shooting he had conducted in Miami. Guess who filed the complaint? The soldiers who rode with him in

Miami. What happened to the loyalty segment of the gang? Their allegation was Sergio had to shoot the weapon multiple times which put them at risk of being noticed or identified by witnesses. The soldiers alleged Sergio had "punked out" and wasn't fit to be a leader. He had been demoted, but was still a leader in the gang. After all, he had been brave enough to take the shot.

When the deputies searched Rita's home, the evidence was definitely in the prosecution's favor. We found the pistol in a safe on a shelf in the closet. There was a phone list labeled "soldiers" on the kitchen counter next to the phone. Included on the list were Jose, and Muerte's numbers. The answering machine even held a piece of the puzzle. One of the soldiers had called on the day we served the search warrants and left a message in Spanish for Rita warning her to leave quickly because the deputies had just picked up one of the soldiers. If it wasn't for the gang agents' surveillance on the apartment, she would have slipped out of town and avoided prosecution. The problem with all of this great evidence is it was what the legal profession calls "circumstantial" evidence. Simply put it means the jury has to decide based on the surrounding circumstances whether there is enough evidence to convince them beyond a reasonable doubt that these five individuals had conspired and attempted to kill Pablo.

Our second big break in the case was a much-needed confession. Guess who broke the code of silence first? Jose! The trash talker and the initiator of the whole incident was the first to snitch on the others. In my opinion he had good cause to cooperate. At seventeen, he was charged with attempted first-degree murder, which was punishable by up to life in prison. In the State of Florida we also have enhanced penalties for gang-related crimes. A jury trial with a conviction would mean at least thirty years in prison for Jose. When Jose's attorney approached me about working out a plea, I was excited! Depending on his testimony, Jose could make our task much easier.

The process of plea negotiations is not as simple as most people think. John and I had to discuss what our options were. The great thing about working in the Ninth Judicial Circuit for the Honorable Lawson Lamar was we were given a lot of discretion. John and I were very honest about our concerns. Our victim was lucky to be alive. It would be an injustice to plea anyone involved in this case to anything less than prison time. The question then became how much prison time followed by what charge would be offered. We decided to offer Jose the deal of his lifetime. If he pled to the charge of attempted second-degree murder, he would serve eight years in prison followed by seven years of probation. We sent the plea offer in writing to his attorney. To our delight, Jose accepted!

The next step is proffering the witness's testimony and offering them immunity for their testimony. This protects both the State and the defendant. By proffering the testimony before we accept his plea, the State ensures the testimony is valuable to our case. The defendant comes in to tell us his side of the story with his attorney present. By offering the defendant immunity, the State promises not to use anything he divulges against him. This allows the State to preview the testimony yet protects the defendant if the State decides the information is not valuable.

The question is why would a defendant tell us the truth or cooperate throughout the whole process? Simple, after the proffer is done on the record, the judge takes the plea of the defendant. However, we don't sentence them until after the conclusion of the other defendant's trials. So if at any time they don't cooperate, the deal is off. If they lie or say something different than what they said in the proffer, they can expect a perjury charge on top of the original charges being reinstated.

With this as the backdrop, John and I proffered Jose. We had an awesome gang unit at the Orange County Sheriff's office. Two of the agents accompanied us for the proffer. We had done our homework. We had very direct questions for Jose. Most importantly, we needed him to tell us who had made the crippling shot from inside the car. We started with simple questions about the gang and his involvement with the gang. Detail by detail he recounted the events leading up to the shooting. There was no remorse in his voice. In his mind, he did what he had to do. He never apologized for the shooting. He had one concern, where would he serve his prison sentence, because his gang would kill him if they located him. He was committing an act of treason by cooperating with the prosecution. We assured him we would do our best to keep him separate from the other members. He made it clear to us the gang was very active in prison. Just as the soldiers acted on command in our case, other members of the gang could kill him in a heart beat if notified to do so.

As harsh as it sounds I could not help thinking; he was not worried about Pablo's life when he involved the soldiers over an argument about a silly bike. But now his life might be at risk, he was worried. I felt a twinge of anger. Jose could walk, could feed himself, could bathe himself, and could brush his teeth, but Pablo couldn't! The sad reality was Jose didn't care about Pablo. He only cared about himself!

As a prosecutor, I have often had to analyze my own feelings and put them in perspective. As I listened to Jose I realized he really was just like everyone else, self-centered. The big difference is most of us do our killing with poison. We use our tongues as our weapons, causing our victims to suffer a slow and painful death. We destroy people with words of anger. We destroy their self-esteem and paralyze them with fear. It is so common in our society, that we get away with what should be a crime! But, we like Jose don't care. All we are concerned with is how other people are affecting us. How do we get our way? How do we get others on our side? When the plan backfires and we have something to lose, then we try to find a way to minimize our involvement and save ourselves.

Jose's concern about his sentence was a valid one. I was glad to know he was human and did have some emotions. I started to ponder how the jury was going to evaluate his testimony. Would his testimony alone be enough to convict Sergio? We would have to think about it and before we could come up with some alternatives, Muerte's attorney contacted us to inform us his client would like to discuss a plea. We offered him the same deal as Jose, eight years in prison followed by seven years on probation. He accepted. Immediately, we set up a proffer with him. Now Muerte's concerns were a little different than Jose's. He was worried about his wife and children. But just like Jose, he never showed any remorse. Muerte had a coldness that could send chills through you. The nickname, angel of death was definitely appropriate for him.

As the trial date grew closer, we had meetings with the defense attorneys to try to negotiate a plea with the two female defendants. We had no success. Their position was simple, they were not present when the shooting took place, and therefore they were not guilty of any crime. In Florida you don't have to be present to be charged with a crime. Any participation, however limited can result in your being charged as a principal in the first degree. The defense attorneys for the three remaining defendants stood their ground. John and I were facing three trials. Sergio and Rita were charged with attempted first-degree murder and Sergio's girlfriend was being tried as an accessory after the fact for helping them escape detection after the shooting.

The trial was going to be challenging. There were three defendants, with two juries. Without making it complicated, if there is going to be testimony from a co-defendant implicating the other defendants, there has to be separate juries. Rita had given what we considered a confession during her interview with the gang agents. Because it implicated Sergio as the shooter, Rita would have her own jury. Sergio and his girlfriend would share a jury. During Rita's taped statement, Sergio's jury would be taken outside of the courtroom for a recess. This would keep her confession from causing undue prejudice to Sergio and his girlfriend.

John and I had our hands full. We were trying to persuade these juries based on the word of two gang members, they had enough evidence to convict the other three. As one of the defense attorneys stated before trial, "It's a matter of credibility." Our justice system says each individual is innocent until proven guilty. This means the State has the burden of proof. John and I divided the witnesses. John would question all of the civilian witnesses. I would question all of the law enforcement officers and co-defendants. We had a file for each witness. We highlighted the key parts of each person's testimony. The police reports were tabbed and highlighted as well. We were organized. We had over thirty pieces of evidence to admit during the trial. We did a chart to help us keep the evidence in order. We wanted this trial to go smoothly.

John did the opening statement. Opening statements are simple and short. As the prosecutors, we tell the jury what we expect our evidence will prove. Then the defense tells their side of the story. Both parties keep it short. No need to bore the jury early in the game. But one thing John had to do was tell the jury up front we had negotiated a plea with two of the defendants. As the State, it is imperative not to hide anything. John told the jury they would hear from Jose and Muerte. He told them about their involvement in the shooting. He told them they would hear about the details of the dispute over the bike and how the gang became involved. They would also hear from Pablo, the victim of this awful drive-by shooting. Almost a year after the shooting we were finally seeking justice on his behalf.

The individual testimony went quickly, we started with Trevor. He had moved out of state after the shooting for fear of retaliation. We had Pablo testify next. The courtroom was solemn and silent as the court deputy pushed Pablo in a special wheel chair in to the courtroom. The jury stared at his limp body-sitting upright in the wheel chair. As he began to describe for the jury how the defendants had changed his life forever, Rita began to cry. John and I both looked at her without sympathy. Did she care when she orchestrated the incident? No! I have often thought that choosing the pistol over the shotgun would have probably changed the nature of the injury to Pablo. One simple act on her part could have changed history. But like so many of us, she just went along with the powers that be. Now, she found herself fighting for her own freedom.

As the testimony continued, one by one law enforcement officers and civilian witnesses recounted what they saw, heard and did on the day Pablo was shot. It was a three-day trial. Piece by piece the evidence was introduced to the jury. The jury was shown pictures of the crime scene, bullets, the pistol, clothing and the shotgun. It seemed as if we had presented a strong case against each of the three defendants by the time we rested our case. The judge jarred our confidence early on and shocked us by acquitting Maria (Sergio's girlfriend) in a motion hearing during the trial.

The motion is called a directed verdict of acquittal. Simply explained, it asks the judge to find the State has failed to prove an essential element of the crime against the defendant and therefore the case is not strong enough to go to a jury. The defense for Maria argued we had not proved Maria's knowledge of the shooting, which is essential to prove the accessory after the fact charge. We had to prove:

> 1. An attempted first degree murder was committed by the co-defendants. (We did that.)

2. After the attempt to commit murder, Maria maintained, assisted, or gave any other aid to the defendants.

3. At the time, Maria knew the co-defendants had attempted the murder.

4. She assisted or gave aid with the intent to help them avoid escape, detection, arrest, trial or punishment.

I would concede knowledge is an element we had to prove. However, how could she *not* know the three gang members had just committed a crime was our argument to the judge. The soldiers came in her apartment acting nervous according to Muerte and Jose. They were talking low, asked to change clothes, put the shotgun and shells on the counter, and shaved their heads to change their appearance. We also stated Maria knew or should have known her boyfriend was a Vice-President in a gang. Our final argument was this all happened in a very small one bedroom apartment. We reminded the judge, intent is an operation of the mind, therefore it is not always capable of direct and positive proof. Our point was the jury could determine her guilt or innocence based on circumstantial evidence like any other fact in the case.

The defense countered by saying there was no blood on anyone or on the clothing. There was no discussion in her presence about the shooting. Although the shells were out in the open on the counter, the shotgun was unassembled and put in a cardboard box before it was taken into the home. The changing of clothes and shaving certainly could not indicate to a reasonable person that someone had just committed a drive-by shooting. The judge agreed and dismissed the charge. Maria was freed from the ankle bracelet that kept her confined for the past year. The judge's ruling meant Maria's case would not go to the jury. She walked out of the courtroom a free woman.

John and I disagreed with the judge, but had to move on. The one thing that becomes very clear, as a lawyer, you can't and won't win them all! The losses always sting. The positive news was the judge denied the motions for Rita and Sergio finding there was enough evidence to send their case to the jury. The defense's case was short. Sergio exercised his Fifth Amendment right and did not testify. Rita did the same. Her confession had been played for the jury. There wasn't a whole lot to add I guess. In the tape, she said she was scared of the gang. She did give them the gun, but didn't know what they were going to do with it. She was trying to tend to her children, after all there were two kids in the house and she was pregnant. She claimed she wasn't in a position to argue with Sergio or the soldiers.

I am not sure I subscribe to the theory that says cases are won or lost in closing arguments. However, I do believe it is the last opportunity the State has to put the pieces of the puzzle together for the jury. My practice has always been to summarize the story and be honest about the weaknesses in the case. John and I had established early on I would give the closing argument. In this case, there was a lot of information to be sorted through in less than an hour. I would have to give two closing arguments. My mission was to persuade twelve individuals on two separate juries that:

1) These defendants did some act towards committing a first-degree murder that went beyond just thinking or talking about it.
2) The defendants acted with a premeditated design to kill Pablo.
3) The act would have resulted in the death of Pablo, except someone prevented the defendant from killing Pablo or Pablo failed to die as a result of the acts.

The law is often complicated; summarizing it in a clear and concise manner is challenging. Adding the complexity of gang culture made my job even harder. This is an abbreviated version of my closing argument:

Ladies and Gentlemen: In opening statements one defense lawyer said we do know "something" happened on the 27th of March 1997. The State's response to that is no, "something" didn't just happen! Pablo was shot in the neck with a shotgun over a stupid argument with Jose!

This ladies and gentlemen, was a senseless shooting that has left a man paralyzed from the neck down. The State of Florida and

Pablo are not seeking your sympathy today, we are demanding justice!

The defense attorney said in this country we don't assume. He was right, in this country we must prove our case. Mr. Pare' and I promised you in opening statements that every bit of testimony relating to the major facts, those elements which make up the legal definition of attempted first degree murder would be consistent. We have delivered on that promise. There is no need to assume anything.

Everyone agrees:

1) *There was an argument between Trevor and Jose over a stolen bike.*
2) *There was a confrontation in the apartment complex between Pablo, Trevor, and Jose. During this confrontation there were no threats, no weapons and no physical fighting. Just an ugly exchange of words.*
3) *After the verbal confrontation, Jose is told to go get the soldiers.*
4) *Jose goes to the home of Rita, tells her what happened and she summons the soldiers via telephone.*
5) *The soldiers meet at Rita's home. She gives them the shotgun, stating the pistol is registered and can be traced.*
6) *The three men get in a small dark four-door car and drive over to the apartments looking for Trevor and Pablo.*
7) *The soldiers circle the apartment complex five to six times, and Jose points out Pablo to Sergio.*
8) *Finally, there is no question that Pablo was shot in the neck with a 12 gauge shot gun leaving him paralyzed for the rest of his life!*

So my job is to answer questions about the few things there may be some disagreement about. Let's get a couple of things out of the way from the start.

1) *It doesn't matter whether the bike was stolen, sold for $20, or given away because the law does not justify shooting someone over a stolen bike, especially when the people who were in possession of the stolen bike are the ones doing the shooting.*
2) *It doesn't matter who cursed at who first.*
3) *It doesn't matter whether these defendants were a member of the Girl Scouts, Boy Scouts, a bridge club or NETA, shooting a person in the neck over someone asking you what the F_ _ _ you looking at is definitely against the law in this country!*

The bottom line is we have talked about NETA and the gang culture during this trial because these defendants acted the way they did because they were members of the gang. That is why they called the "soldiers" to come and deal with the situation because there is a brotherhood.

So did the State prove our case against the defendants?
1) *Did Sergio do an act toward committing murder that went beyond just thinking or talking about it?*
   a) *He went to Rita's house and got a shotgun! He could have ignored her call, but he doesn't, he responds to it!*
   b) *He provides the car to go to the apartments.*
   c) *He loads the shotgun and puts it together in the car.*
   d) *He takes aim at Pablo and shoots him!*
2) *Did Sergio act with premeditated design to kill Pablo?*
   a) *He got a shotgun although he wasn't involved in the argument.*
   b) *If he is just going to fight or participate in a "beat down" as the gang calls it, why did he need a gun?*
   c) *If he is just going to make a threat or scare Pablo, then why does he load the gun? The answer is simple, he INTENDED to shoot Pablo!*
   d) *He directed them to drive around a couple of times, which means he had more than enough time to think about what he did.*
   e) *And to make matters worse, Sergio aimed the gun at Pablo's head, which means he intended to blow his head off! That ladies and gentlemen is a design to kill!*

The only thing we have left to prove to you is the shot would have resulted in the death of Pablo, except someone prevented Sergio from killing Pablo or that he failed to do so. Emergency surgery is the only thing that saved Pablo's life! If it wasn't for medical miracles and prayers, Sergio would be dead today!

Did the State prove to you Rita did some act toward committing murder that went beyond just talking about it or thinking about it?

1) *We have charged Rita as a principal this means she MUST be treated as if she had done all of the things the other persons did if:*

   a. *She had a conscious intent that the criminal act be done.*

   b. *She did some act or said some word which was intended to aid, incite, cause, encourage, assist or advise the other persons to actually commit or attempt to commit murder.*

   c. *The reality for Rita is she didn't have to call anybody, in fact, she didn't have to let the guys in her house at all. There was no reason for her to get involved in this situation! She could have said, guys this is your problem. You call! And not from my house! Go to your own house and make plans! I don't want to be involved.*

   d. *But by her own words she admits, that SHE called Sergio because she knew Sergio would know what to do with the guys.*

   e. *Ladies and Gentlemen: I'm going to be honest, the fact that she was pregnant doesn't mean a thing, because her actions were not consistent with a scared little pregnant woman!*

   f. *She never appeared to be scared of Sergio. She wasn't afraid to call him and get him involved or tell him what was going on. She brought this on herself because she calls the guys. In the taped interview she tells the gang agent, NOBODY made her call, she DID IT ON HER OWN!*

   g. *The other problem with her testimony is despite saying in court she told Sergio she wouldn't give him the gun, her* action of letting him in the house after he tells her on the phone he wants the shotgun, the pistol or whatever just doesn't make sense. She wants you to believe she is afraid of Sergio, but in the same breath she trusted him enough to call him to handle the situation. The bottom line is she trusted him enough to let him in her house, the one place she had the power to take control of the situation.

h. Don't be fooled, Rita knew Sergio had the power to call the shots! She knew he could order a beat down or an execution. So when she made the call to Sergio she had the power of life and death in HER hands.

i. The defense says Rita was just an innocent bystander in the whole situation. This is interesting because their theory is Rita had to call Sergio because he was second in command of NETA. He was the one making the decisions not Rita.

j. Think about this: just because a person is a member of the Elks Club with hundreds of other people doesn't mean you invite the chain of command to your home, especially when you claim you don't get along with them.

k. Rita alleged she was afraid of Sergio BUT:

   1) She says he always comes over and goes through their stuff. If he always does this and it upsets her then why did she call him and let him in her house? It doesn't make sense!

   2) Sergio had the key to the gun box that was kept at her house...why?

   3) Sergio didn't take the pistol because Rita told him it was registered. So what stopped her from telling him not to take the shotgun or refusing to give him access to the guns?

   4) What Rita did, was tell Sergio to take the shotgun and Ladies and Gentleman, that is when she had the power of life or death. She chose death right along with everyone else in this case.

a. Rita wants you to believe she thought the guys were just going to fight, but if it was just going to be a fight then *why did they need a gun and why was she concerned about the pistol being registered and traced back to her?*

b. *There is an instruction the judge will read dealing with abandonment: Rita could have abandoned this deal on more than one occasion.*

1) *She could have anonymously called the police when the guys left and foiled their plan. She could have given them the description of the car or the tag number, or told them to hurry over to the apartment complex because someone was about to be shot.*

2) *She could have warned the soldiers not to go.*

3) *But instead of trying to help another human being, she runs out of the apartment with a suitcase trying to hide the gangs paperwork!*

4) *The bottom line is she did not have to be involved at all.*

5) *The law says she doesn't have to be present when the murder is attempted! It's clear, Rita did some act toward committing the attempted murder that went beyond just talking or thinking about it. The final question is can you believe the codefendants who testified for the State, Muerte and Jose? They both turned themselves in. They didn't have to. They both told you the same thing about the major events in this story. They are both going to prison for eight years followed by seven years of probation. They are both facing death because they have violated the norms of the gang by speaking to the police. And as they said, "by testifying in this trial we have risked our lives to tell you what happened that day." It was Jose that helped the gang agents solve this case.*

Muerte is twenty years old and has never been convicted of a felony. He has a wife and a child. Yet he came forward and admitted he was wrong. He could have gone to Puerto Rico to hide. There is no doubt about it, we would have had a hard time finding him. But he didn't do that. Despite knowing his image would not be favorable, he told you his nickmame is death and showed you his tattoo of the angel of death on his arm. He was forthright and you must weigh that in your deliberations.

Jose is only eighteen, but has been convicted of theft, burglary, and carrying a weapon to school. He was honest with you about his criminal background. He admitted he was in a gang but more importantly he knew this shooting was wrong. Everything he told the officers was verified. He led the officers to the gun, the clothes and each of the houses that were involved.

Both told you the truth and said no one hit them in the original confrontation. No one threatened them. No one had any weapons. They could have lied, made up a story and said that they were in fear for their lives and that is why they went to get the soldiers. They both admit they could have stopped the shooting...but did not. For that there is no excuse and that is why they are going to prison!

Now the question is will Sergio and Rita be held responsible for their part in this tragic and senseless shooting of a thirty-two year old man? The State challenges you to do the right thing today! Hold Sergio and Rita responsible for their role in this drive-by shooting. We have proven the elements as required by law. We have produced thirty-three pieces of evidence, including the weapon, sixteen witnesses and more importantly statements from the defendants' own mouths. We have done our job, now it is up to you. Pablo, along with myself and Mr. Pare' aren't asking you for your sympathy, we are asking you for justice!!!

We are confident you will return the only just verdict in this case, a verdict of guilty for attempted first degree murder! Thank you.

I have always said I am not sure that you win or lose a case in closing argument. But what I do believe is it provides you one last opportunity to persuade your jury that justice is in their hands. I make eye contact with each juror. I try to establish a connection with them that makes them feel what I am saying. As I sat down, John gave me his sign of approval. The two defense attorneys argued on behalf of their clients' innocence. Sergio's lawyer argued no one other than the co-defendants could prove his identity. In his opinion, they were not credible witnesses because they cut a deal with the government to save their own behinds. All the government had was circumstantial evidence against Sergio and in his opinion that was not enough to convict his client.

Rita's attorney argued she was a victim of circumstance. She was a scared mother who just did what she was told. She was under duress when the guys started showing up and had no clue what was going on. She wasn't there when the shooting occurred. So how could she be liable for this tragedy. I know I must have been rolling my eyes and my whole demeanor must have said, "Give me a break!"

At the conclusion of the closing arguments the judge read the jury instructions, which is one of the most boring, but important parts of the trial. John and I read along in our copy of the Florida Laws and Rules of Criminal Procedure Manual. Once the judge finished almost thirty minutes later the court deputy escorted the jury out.

The courtroom was quite busy with the victim's family asking us questions. All of the gang agents had attended closing arguments. They were really one of the best groups of specialized units I have ever worked with. They told John and I they would be there until the verdicts came back. There was one other key guest in the audience. The State President of the gang had joined us. He was Rita's husband. I can remember him just staring at John and I. He had a strong, quiet presence. But his mission was clear. He wanted us to know he was there. He wanted our witnesses to know he was there. When I gave my argument, I looked over at him to let him know I have a strong presence as well. I was not intimidated. John sure wasn't intimidated. (Not to mention we were in a courtroom full of court deputies and gang agents.)

An hour and twenty-six minutes later Rita's jury knocked on the door to signify they had reached a verdict. My heart started beating. My nerves always get jittery during the formality of the verdicts. It only takes a few seconds, but the sentence seems to take forever.

The clerk read the verdict, "We the jury, find the defendant, NOT GUILTY of attempted first degree murder." Rita started crying at the realization she was free. I was in disbelief! John simply said he was disappointed by the verdict. Rita was the one person who had the opportunity to stop this horrible crime, but she didn't. In fact she facilitated it. But the jury didn't see fit to punish her. I agreed with John's position wholeheartedly! I was very disappointed!

Sergio's jury was still deliberating. John and I had to make rounds with the victim's family and the agents to discuss Rita's verdict while assuring them, Sergio's verdict would be different. These were two totally separate juries. I was getting a little nervous the jury was taking so long. Justice demanded Sergio be found guilty! Once you get a not guilty verdict, your mind starts to race. I asked John if he had any doubt we would get the conviction on Sergio. He said no. His response made me feel a little better. But I tell you, you never know until you hear the words from the clerk's mouth.

Thirty minutes after Rita's verdict, there was a knock at the door to indicate the second jury had reached a verdict. I almost wanted to reach over and hold John's hand. Instead I took a deep breath and held it. The foreperson handed the sealed envelope to the court deputy. The jury would not look at John and I. This made me nervous. When the judge took the verdict form out of the envelope to make sure it was filled out properly, I couldn't read his face either. He handed it to the clerk and eternity started all over again.

The clerk read the verdict, "We the Jury find the defendant guilty of the lesser included offense of attempted second degree murder." In plain English, what the jury did was give Rita a jury pardon, then give Sergio the same level offense as his co-defendants that cut a deal. John and I decided they probably thought if we offered the two snitches attempted second degree murder, then it was only fair to give Sergio the same level of offense. Our rationale, was Jose and Muerte did not pull the trigger therefore attempted second degree murder was justifiable. But Sergio should have been convicted of the attempted first degree murder. Our rationale didn't matter at this point, the jury had spoken. We had to honor the verdict.

In the State of Florida you can seek enhancements for certain crimes. John and I had already filed a motion to enhance the penalties if Sergio was convicted on the basis he was in a criminal street gang. The judge delayed the sentencing for two months and set the motion for hearing. This would be the first adult gang enhancement in the history of the Ninth Judicial Circuit.

On my twenty-eighth birthday I sat with the Honorable Lawson Lamar who was the State Attorney for the entire Ninth Judicial Circuit on my left side and John Pare' on my right side. The hearing lasted almost two days. It was a mini trial with the gang agents testifying all over again about the evidence. We had to prove this was a criminal street gang. Muerte and Jose testified again about the gang's structure, membership and activity. Although the victim was present we did not need him to testify. The media had come out for phase two of this high-publicity case. At the conclusion of the hearing, the State was granted the enhancement which took Sergio's sentence from a high of fifteen years in prison to a sentence of twenty-nine years for the shooting. The victim was pleased, so was the gang agents from the Sheriff's office. Justice prevailed.

As Sergio walked out of the courtroom, he showed his lack of remorse one more time. He shed no tears, showed no shock and definitely gave no apology. The cameras were rolling and he needed people to know he was true to the gang until the end. With his hands in cuffs, he lifted them up and formed the gang's sign. I immediately thought, "What a true punk! While you are serving your twenty-nine years, nobody is going to care about your gang!"

Different reporters were interviewing agents or the victim. When I walked out of the courtroom several reporters asked me for a statement. I like to keep statements for the media simple. As a communications major I know what they are looking for is a good sound bite. Something short, sweet and to the point. I told the reporters, "We aren't going to take it anymore! We aren't going to let these gangs destroy our communities."

Before John and I left the courthouse, we said a final good bye to the victim and his family. My heart was heavy with sadness. This had been a long battle for all of us. As he was saying thank you to us, I was thinking, "here I am at the conclusion of another major trial with no idea of what is going to happen to my victim in the future." I bent down to give Pablo a hug. Everything in me realized how one moment, one argument, had changed this man's life forever.

I talked with Pablo off and on over the course of the next year. He was in physical therapy and doing relatively well. He experienced struggles with depression. But what really surprised me was he had not heard from Trevor since the trial. Trevor hadn't called to check on his progress at all! Wow, how incredible! Pablo's life had been changed forever by him standing up for Trevor's stolen bike and now the question was, "Who cares?"

I can't help but wonder how we as humans become so selfish. Why do we fail to show our appreciation when others show acts of kindness towards us? Why don't we care when others are hurting? Why don't we acknowledge the good in people instead of focusing on the negative? Why do we get a gang mentality when we are in trouble and want to pull people in to help us fight our battles? We get on the phone and start talking to our friends. We tell them what someone has done to us. We look for reassurance that we have a reason to be upset, hurt, or disappointed. I know because I am guilty!

The final verdict in this life will be, who cares about you and who did you care about? The September 11, 2001 attack on the World Trade Centers taught the United States of America that office size, salary, or how many hours you work really doesn't matter. So many of us are fighting battles that are stealing our energy and our life. The soldiers in this case fought for what seemed like a good cause when they were summoned. It appeared to be a battle about honor. It was really a battle over power and ego. The battle cost them some of the most valuable years in their life.

What are you fighting for? And in the end will it matter? Are you working long hours and neglecting your family so you can get promoted? If the answer is yes, will the promotion balance out in the long run or will it be a series of events stealing years from your life. I'm all for financial stability and freedom. However, I am a firm believer in taking time to enjoy what you are working for. When you are gone, how many hours you worked will not be etched on your tombstone.

Whom are you picking arguments with and why? I'd be willing to bet a thousand dollars Trevor had no idea what an argument would cost him or Pablo. Who cares that your co-worker gets on your nerves? Who cares about the dishes not being washed or as one lady in a stress management seminar after the September 11th tragedy told me, "My husband doesn't fold the laundry right!" I along with almost every other woman in the room immediately commented, "You should be happy your husband does the laundry!"

Who cares who started a rumor about you? Who cares who's talking about you behind your back? If they are not big enough to talk to you about their concern, or ask you what they want to know, they are showing you who they are. Believe them! They are people with no life and no courage. So leave them where they are! You are on your way to your destiny and each day you spend dealing with trivial things is a day you loose. It is a day you could have utilized to get you one step closer to your dream.

So many of us pick fights over minimal things or situations. I've done it! I still do it! But when I find myself getting bent out of shape I ask the extremely difficult question: **"Who really cares?"** This helps me put things in a different perspective. Normally it creates a sense of calm where there was a sense of urgency or frustration. I take it one step further and ask what is this situation going to benefit or cost me? This is when the true essence of the matter becomes clear. I can see the big picture when I ask this question. I can find the ability to walk away, be still, or the really hard one for me, be quiet! I can create my destiny and my peace by going back to the basics: I am only responsible for me. If I make good choices, I will experience good consequences. This will allow me to affect others in a positive way.

When you show people how much you care, they start caring about you. Remember I started this chapter off by explaining the reasons gangs are alive and well is because they provide an environment of caring. The members provide basics like food, shelter and clothing. They take care of one another in difficult situations which builds allegiance to the gang. When the gang calls on them, they are willing to risk their lives and freedom to protect the gang.

I am now a loyal member of John's gang. I say this with a smile. But I am very sincere in my loyalty to him and his journey. John has been one of my biggest supporters. John and his wife, Pam are an amazing couple. They have supported me in every major event in my life since I met them. I attended their wedding. They attended my first book release. They believe in my dream. But more importantly they believe in me as an individual. John is very intelligent and continues to guide me in my business endeavors. John is now an in-house lawyer for a major corporation in Central Florida. Although we don't work in the same office, we are still partners. I know when I need him, he is just a call or email away. I know he will show up to fight life's battles with me.

When my mother died in 2002, I sent out one of my motivational thoughts via email entitled, "What if tomorrow never comes?" I included information about the funeral at the conclusion of the email because so many people had asked and I couldn't return all the phone calls. I was overwhelmed by the attendance of so many friends, associates, students and co-workers. I was standing at the door of the church greeting those who had come to honor my mother's life with our family when I saw this handsome FBI looking guy walk through the door. Tears swelled in my eyes as he came closer. It was one of my soldiers. It was John! He'd kill me if I told you why his attendance was so major for both of us. But I'll say this, I hadn't called John. I hadn't asked him to come. In fact, I would have never guessed he would attend. He had already sent a donation in my mother's honor to the American Cancer Society. John didn't know my mother. The service was on a Friday which meant, he had to take off from work to attend.

I gave John a huge hug as he walked in the sanctuary. By now I was crying. His support during the loss of my mother showed me how much he really cared. John doesn't show very many emotions. But his presence is powerful and very calming to me. He sat right behind me during the service. As we left the church to go to the cemetery he gave me another hug. He had to go back to work. As soon as I got home, I called John at the office. I started out by thanking him for coming. I followed by telling him I was doing well as a greeter until I saw him walk through the door. How dare he make me cry! I turned my attention to the real reason for my call: "Why had he come?" This may seem like a silly question, but I'm sure you all know someone who doesn't do funerals for a variety of reasons.

John's response caused the tears to start streaming from my eyes again. "Veraunda, I came because I care about you, I wanted to be there with you." "But John," I responded, "I would have never guessed in a thousand years you would have shown up at the church!"

He responded, "You are one of those people that people want to be there for." I was touched.

A month or so later, John and his wife invited me out to dinner. They were expecting their first child. I, of course, was excited about becoming an aunt, so we talked a lot about the pregnancy. I suggested the baby have at least "V" somewhere as a middle name if it was a girl. Olivia Veraunda Pare' has a nice ring to it. We laughed.

I believe in speaking your future in the present. We chatted a little about the mega empire my company was becoming and how I would need a good lawyer. I have often said I can't think of a better person to represent me than John. I had sent him a copy of Oprah on the cover of Fortune 500. I took the liberty of highlighting some important areas for his review. The areas I highlighted dealt with how Oprah had formed a powerful team of people she trusted. More importantly, she surrounded herself with people who believed in her vision and her value. John recited one of his favorite lines from the movie, Jerry McGuire, "Veraunda, show me the money!" We laughed again.

We closed the conversation about my reality that I had some estate planning I needed to handle. My mother's death was a reminder life is short. I told John and Pam, I had come to realize it was a good possibility my sorority would have to be responsible for my funeral service because my immediate family is so small. If my father and grandmother predecease me, that is it for my blood relatives who would know me well enough to bury me. By now tears were forming again. I continued by saying, I was trying to prepare for the holidays without my mother. It would be hard. John reached across the table and gently took my hand in his. As I spoke he rubbed my hand. His face showed his concern. Without hesitation, John said, "Veraunda, you are a part of our family." I felt John's sincerity and was comforted by his words. As I drove home that evening, I recall thinking, "If John never said the words, "I love you, Veraunda" his actions have said it on more than one occasion. I know without doubt he cares!

To some extent, I believe we are all a part of a gang. We are all trying to build a support network with other humans that will allow us to be loved unconditionally. We crave for genuine concern from our friends and loved ones. A word of caution, choose the members of your gang carefully. Refuse to allow them to pull you into a situation without knowing the consequences. If they show you they are not trustworthy, believe them! If they show you they don't care, believe them! If they show you they are not reliable, believe them! *Care enough about yourself* to see the truth in every situation.

Figure out what is important to you and how you can accomplish your life's vision. Look at the people in your life, who's helping you make the vision a reality? Who is criticizing your vision? Who simply doesn't care about your vision?

I wonder what would have happened in March of 1997 if Rita would have chosen not to care about a stupid argument over a bike? If she had asked herself, "Who cares if Trevor was rude?" If she had said, "Nope, not my problem and I'm not going to allow you to alter my destiny by pulling me into your ridiculous issues!" My educated guess is life would have been very different for at least Rita, maybe even Pablo and the rest of the gang. Just maybe her decision to not care about trivial issues would have changed the whole course of events!

The two women in my case ended up with freedom from the criminal justice system. But they both lost almost eighteen valuable months of their lives locked down on house arrest because they allowed other people to convince them to get involved in a matter that had absolutely nothing to do with their life's vision. I wonder what their dream was? What did they want to do when they were little kids? How did they get so off track? How did they wind up in relationships with gang members who didn't care? But more importantly, how did they wind up not caring enough about themselves to see the truth in the situation?

It is sad so many people lose sight of their vision. We don't grow up thinking about being a criminal. When we blow out our candles on the cake, we don't wish to be arrested for violating the law or to be a victim of a tragedy. But when we allow others to pull us into their fights, their poverty, their lack of self-esteem, their lack of faith and courage, we end up pleading for our own survival. We get sucked into their nine-to-five office mentality. We get pulled into their box of limitations and ocean of fears. We get swept up in their constant drama. Then we wonder why we aren't happy? Why we aren't fulfilled and most importantly, why our associates, friends and family *don't seem to care about us.*

Start asking the people around you about their vision. What do they see for themselves? You will be amazed at how many people have never seriously articulated their vision. Many people have been laughed at or put down for having a vision, so they abandoned the vision for people who could care less about their well-being and success. When you start seeing and believing in their vision, most people will start seeing and believing in your vision. Start encouraging those who are serious to have the courage to act on their vision. For those who are scared or have lost sight of their vision due to their membership in a negative gang, reassure them dreams don't die, people do! Keep in mind it is their choice to care enough about themselves to see the truth in every situation. Please, if you can't help someone with their vision, don't dare hurt them in the pursuit of their vision! Just walk away!

Start creating options in your own life. The first step is figuring out who really cares and caring enough about yourself, to see the truth in every situation! So who cares? *You* should care about you enough to not only believe in your vision, but to make the vision a reality, despite the many gangs that will try to recruit you in pursuit of your dreams. It's simple, *who cares* depends on who you hang out with and how much *you* care about you!

Apply the lesson in this chapter to your life:

What battle are you fighting that has nothing to do with you?

Who are the people <u>you</u> really care about?

Who are the people who will support you unconditionally in the pursuit of your vision?

Are you doing all you can to support those around you in the pursuit of their vision?

It's Only Temporary!

A year and six months after starting my company, EHAP Inc., I found myself in a huge dilemma. Operating a company is always a challenge financially for the first few years. I had done my homework before jumping out into the sea of entrepreneurship. I had spoken with an accountant before I ventured out on this great journey. He warned me, "The average company loses money the first two years." His advice was to keep working as long as I could to offset the startup expenses. As a speaker and a writer, you have to promote yourself in addition to the book. This means, traveling, mailing and networking on a continuous basis. How do you do this while working full- time as an attorney? As a prosecutor it would be even harder because we are in court daily. After careful consideration, I decided to resign from my full time position as an Assistant State Attorney and follow my dreams.

You must understand this company was a total leap of faith. According to the Florida Bar, 88% of all the lawyers in Florida were making at least $50,000 a year in 2001. Prior to leaving the government, I was a part of that 88%. I didn't have any idea how much money I could make, but I did know eventually I would be wealthy. I had visions of helping others in the form of scholarships and charitable donations. I wanted to clear out my debt, especially my $88,000 with interest in student loans. Working for a company, or in my case, the government, means you have a salary limit. The top official in my office was making a little over six figures. In 1999, over 56% of lawyers were making more than $100,000 a year. I definitely was not in that percentage. I was settling for much less than I was worth. To make it to six figures as a prosecutor, I would have to stay at least ten years. Instead, I resigned with less than six years with the government.

Logic told me that when you own your own company, the sky is the limit. I could be a best-selling author, and a world-renowned speaker! I could be wealthy and provide blessings for others. Now let me be clear, I loved my job as a prosecutor. I loved the ability I had to make a positive impact in the lives of others, but I was settling for making a few dollars and making a difference in a few lives. Speaking gave me the possibility to make more and do more. It wasn't just the possibility of making money. It was the possibility of making a difference in the lives of millions by doing what I loved. I could travel the world! I tell you the "possibilities" were exciting!

Reality said patience is a virtue. At thirty-one years old with a law degree, I sat in the Whitehall Staffing office almost in disbelief a year and a half after starting the company. I was filling out an application and listing my clerical skills. I was applying for temporary office work. In all honesty, my attitude was that I am or at least *should be* beyond this. (Please note I did not say *above*, instead I purposely chose the word *beyond*, which signifies past this stage in my life.) My mind kept reflecting on the fact that I had a secretary at twenty-three years old. Even interns in law school had secretaries! Now here I was applying to go in and out of offices to fill in for receptionists, clerks and secretaries. Your thoughts can manipulate your progress if you are not careful. I had to get a grip quickly. I was in a financial crunch and regardless of what my ego said, reality was crystal clear...I needed money!

There were some slow periods I hadn't prepared for. I used my credit cards to start the company. When things got rough, I used the credit cards to cover expenses. But the credit cards only lasted so long. I charged my credit cards to the limit trying to finance my dream. I didn't want to take out a business loan. After my divorce I vowed to avoid creating new debt especially in the form of bank loans. To be honest, I probably would not have qualified with my debt-to-income ratio. The creditors were calling daily. The mortgage company had sent a letter indicating my home was going into default. I was requesting extensions monthly for my utilities and phone service. Even the ability to buy food became scarce. There were many days that gas money was a miracle, or two dollars got me from one destination to the next.

The one thing I want you to understand is that my company was doing well. I wasn't a failure by any definition. I was selling books and speaking all over the country. Money was coming in each month, but not enough to cover my expenses. I had a huge amount of debt, and just because I was making money doesn't mean that everything was fine. I had my personal expenditures and the business expenses. The financial side of business is the hardest part. I had invested my own money to start this company. So with the company as my only source of income, paying me a salary was last on the list of priorities.

When you own a company you invoice clients. Often it takes thirty to sixty days after the service has been rendered to receive payment. By the time you receive the payment, bills are past due and the next month's statements are stacking up. The real problem is you have no guarantee of when or how much you will be paid. When I worked for the government, my check was direct deposited on the last working day of the month. ALWAYS! I knew exactly how much my check would be. Well, when you own a private company, you are at the mercy of those purchasing your products or services. We are not taught these kinds of business issues in college. Law school professors never mentioned the day-to-day operations of owning a business. We are just taught to follow your dream. But let me tell you, following your dream is serious business!

I had no health insurance for almost two years. My savings account was depleted. I invested my deferred compensation from the State of Florida into the company. When I didn't work, I didn't get a check. It was just that simple. There was no sick or vacation time. After thirteen years of excellent credit, I had bills thirty to sixty days past due. I was frustrated by the delinquency of my bills, but I knew this situation was only temporary. I had read about other wealthy and famous people. I used their stories to encourage me through the process. I knew about them struggling to make their dreams a reality. The stories of well-known people include extreme hardships like living on the street or waiting on tables to pay the rent while they auditioned for movie roles. No matter what the hardship, each beamed uncontrollably when they told the story. The stories all ended with: "Yes, I had to struggle to get here, but look at me now! I made it and it is worth every bit of the struggle I had to endure." These stories reminded me I would be fine in the long run. In the meantime, I had to find a way to generate income without giving up on my dream.

A friend who had started her own company about the same time as I did suggested temping. Temping is working for companies who may be short on staff or have employees out on leave. Your assignments are given on a daily or weekly basis. The most important thing is that you get paid weekly. It is amazing how we always think we are the only ones going through a difficult time or circumstance. My friend happened to be experiencing a lot of the same challenges that I was as a new business owner. She explained that temping provided flexibility because the agency works around your schedule and the pay was decent ranging from $8 - $10 per hour. When most lawyers are making over $200 an hour, decent is relative. I wasn't thrilled about the idea of temping, but I didn't have a lot of options at this point.

After I completed the application, I was taken to a small computer room for a typing and basic computer skills test. HA!!! I hadn't taken a typing test since my seventh grade typing class! I kept saying, "this is CRAZY, Veraunda!!!" Well, the good news is I learned I typed an average of sixty words per minute. Not bad for a novice. I was impressed.

I was given an orientation session by Jill. She asked me what my goal was and what kind of work I was looking for. Good question! On the one hand, I didn't want to be here at all. On the other hand, I needed the money! How do you explain that tactfully? I gave her a general explanation of my background: I was an attorney, I started my own company, and I needed temporary income to bridge the financial gap. With that out of the way, she went over the dress code, reporting procedures and explained pay dates were every Friday. Now that was good news.

I felt like I had two different people in my head. For entertainment purposes only, (*some people will suggest I have mental issues, but I assure you I am fine! In no way are the names or attitudes I*

describe a reflection of ethnic stereotyping, just my imagination at work).
I will give them names and describe their personalities for you:

Keisha is African American with a serious pride problem. She doesn't believe she is negative, instead she prefers to see her remarks as keeping it real. She is often talking in a firm tone. Keisha is no-nonsense, very impatient and very direct. She wants us to succeed, but prefers the stability in the comfort zone.

Lucy is Latin, has a wonderful accent and a soft, soothing voice. She is well-versed in life lessons and knows that patience is a virtue. Lucy is firmly grounded in her faith. She is full of confidence and trusts the process of life. You can hear the smile in her voice. Lucy believes if we just keep traveling in a forward direction and stay focused we can't lose. Lucy is diligent and has a spirit of perseverance. With the descriptions in place, here is what was going on in my head.

Lucy: Veraunda, it is all right; it is only temporary! Temping doesn't mean you failed, it only means you have the courage to be honest with yourself and realize you need to bridge your financial gap. What would constitute failure is if you gave up on your dream.

Keisha: Girl, are you kidding me?!? You didn't spend seven years in college to temp!!! Just think about what you are doing!!! You are going to work in clerical positions for eight to ten dollars an hour. You make three times that amount teaching one hour. (I hated math in school, but Keisha seemed to be able to come up with all kinds of calculations without any effort.)

Lucy: It could be worse, you know. At least you are working in offices, in the cool air conditioning. Remember, what you are telling everyone else around the country, do what you have to do, to get where you need to be. Right now, you need to make your financial ends meet. Temping is a very realistic and viable way to fill this need and it will still allow you to run your company. Veraunda, it is all right because it is only temporary!

Keisha: You can listen to Lucy if you want to, but the numbers are the numbers!

-If you sell one book that is sixteen dollars, which equals two hours of work.

- You make fifty to one hundred times that when you speak for just an hour.

-One week of temping will barely pay your car note. Shoot, after taxes it won't pay your car note.

-Girl, just call the State Attorney's Office, you know you can go back to practicing law. In one month, you will be out of debt and back on your feet. You can worry about this speaking and book thing later. This temping is definitely not what you went to school for! It is a waste of your time and certainly a waste of your talent!

Lucy: Going back to the State Attorney's office is not going to fulfill you. It'll solve your money problems, but what about all of your "possibilities?" What about living your dreams? You'll go back and get stuck. You'll get comfortable. You'll get stuck in fear. Fear of not making it again, fear of resigning a second time. Fear of what people think. Veraunda, your dream IS becoming a reality every day you hang in there. This place of financial instability is ONLY temporary!

Keisha had no response to that one! It's amazing how life will answer your questions if you allow it. I knew deep down inside Keisha was dead wrong and Lucy was absolutely right. Keisha's attitude would cause me to lose everything I had. Be clear, I'm not talking about losing my material possessions. Rather, I am talking about my most treasured possession, *my dream!* Lucy, had summed it up nicely: the situation was only temporary.

My first assignment was a week of half days for a local homebuilder. It was a beautiful office with warm, friendly people. Thank goodness! I had no idea what to expect. Keisha talked to me the entire drive on the first day.

Keisha: These people will have no idea who you are! Girl, you have more education than most of them. Why are you doing this?

Lucy: Keisha, be quiet! Veraunda, these people are asking for a temp because they need help. You will be fine.

Keisha: *Girl, I don't know why you listen to her! Don't humiliate us like this. Please just go back to being a lawyer. The money is a hundred times better and you'll have your own office and your own secretary. You don't have to answer phones for other people. What if you are filing all day? You better rethink this!*

What Keisha was really saying was I should be too proud to temp. Working for the government, I had never worked with a temp or at least if I had, I didn't know it. I had no clue what I would be doing. Perhaps filing? Maybe answering phones? Now, that would be a trip. Me on a switchboard? Keisha had a good point: I had never operated multiple phone lines. I barely knew how to transfer calls from my desk as an attorney.

Lucy: *This is not humiliating. It is a life lesson you will be able to share with others. Not to mention you are going to learn some valuable office skills. Remember when you were a little girl pretending to be a receptionist? Think of the positives: you are going to have a steady paycheck and meet some people who might be able to enhance your speaking career. Remember, it is only temporary!*

Perhaps you have some voices in your head telling you what to do. They are usually very different voices. No matter what names you give them, they are normally at odds. One voice is very strong and quite boisterous. It is the one that wants to keep you in a sense of panic and hysteria. The other voice is a softer, wiser and calming voice. I am learning to listen to the voice of calm. In most cases it will lead you in the right direction. This is the voice telling you everything will be ok; take life one day at a time.

On my first day as a temp, every person who walked in the door greeted me with a friendly hello. They introduced themselves. Keisha was definitely wrong. No one treated me like I was any different than the full-time employees. I had a wonderful trainer who showed me how to operate the phone system. In fact, she had been a temp before being offered the receptionist job full-time. All of the fears were gone one hour into the first day. The first week passed quickly. The supervisor asked me to come back at the end of the month to fill in for the receptionist again. This was a positive sign. I was feeling a little better about my decision to seek out temporary employment. But wait, you haven't heard about the second week.

Have you ever had a positive experience and started feeling really good about your decision when suddenly a negative door slams the good right out? Well, my second week of temping almost pushed me over the edge. I was excited because it was a forty-hour week for a government agency. The excitement flew out of the window thirty minutes into the job.

I was greeted and given the introductory tour of the office. I was seated in a cubicle area where I would spend the next five days imaging. This is a fancy way to say I would be sitting at a desk for eight hours a day scanning tons of documents into the computer. Talk about bored out of my mind! I wanted to scream! You know who appears at this point.

Keisha: Girl, I told you! But noooo, you want to listen to Miss Calm and Collective. You are going to loose your mind here. If I were you, I would just go ahead and work till the end of the day, then don't come back. See, this is just one example of why you should call your old office and go back. I'm telling you one word comes to mind...WASTE!

Lucy: It's not that bad, trust me. It could be worse, it is a paycheck and it is not hard work.

Keisha: Sure isn't hard, a four-year-old child could do this with no problem. Hello!!! We are talking college-educated woman here. Why am I the only one who sees a problem here?

Lucy: Cause you are the only one who seems to have an attitude and an ego! We are not here for a permanent position, we are here as a bridge over financial instability. We are just crossing this place to get to a better place. Veraunda, it's not going to kill you, it's only temporary.

Keisha: Keep listening to her, and she is going to have you going crazy. I am telling you ditch this place quickly!

I have to tell you by the first break at ten that morning, I was ready to cry! I felt like a complete loser. My pride was killing me. The time was passing VERY slowly. I was questioning my decisions and my dreams. How was I going to get through this financial drought? Just one good speaking engagement could catch up my bills overnight. Why did I have to go through this? It wasn't fair! Yada, yada, yada! You know the lines because you have probably said them to yourself every time the road gets rocky. It is a series of woe-is-me lines which I guarantee can make you lose focus and destroy you if you aren't careful.

When I went back to my cubicle, the supervisor was the bearer of good news. She said, "Some of the girls get bored, so you are free to listen to a Walkman or the radio if you have a headset." Now that was music to my ears, literally! I had a Walkman in my car and you best believe I brought it back with me after lunch. This made the scanning a little less painful. I decided to listen to a motivational tape. Lord knows I needed it. It lifted my spirits and got me through the first day. I called the temp agency to tell them this assignment was not challenging and inquired about another assignment. They did not have anything at the moment, but they would let me know if something else opened up. Great! So here are the options, stay here and get a paycheck or go home and not eat. Hmmm, hard choice. I stayed but vowed at the end of the week, come hell or high water, I was out of there.

When life gets rough, we have choices. Usually they are not very difficult. Either do what you have to do to get where you want to be or wallow and drown in self-pity. I don't know about you, but drowning is not an option for me. To stay afloat, all I needed was a reality check. The big picture held a promise of financial prosperity and freedom. A reality check is often as simple as looking at how far you have come so you can see progress. Sometimes, looking at the distance of your future can be overwhelming and restricting.

I had done quite well in my first year of business. I did not borrow any money to start the company. I hadn't lost anything of value despite my financial woes, so it wasn't as bad as it seemed. Other than a few close friends, the rest of the world had no clue how much I was struggling at times. I was choosing to focus on the positive instead of crying about the negative.

Every day when I went to the government office, I took two motivational tapes. One tape carried me through the morning, and one tape made the afternoon bearable. I listened to classical music in between the tapes for a soothing ambiance. To survive the week, I changed my mindset and surrounded myself with audio motivation. Believe it or not, the job got better. What a tough lesson to digest! You've heard it before: your thoughts can determine your outcomes. Once I had my mind under control, things were not as bad as they had appeared. It did not change the fact that I was bored, nor did it change the amount of pay I was getting. What it did do, was get me *through* the experience. I survived the week but decided one week was more than enough! When Friday came, I was out of there!

Here's the kicker, while I was temping, I received several inquiries about speaking. The business was coming in slowly but surely, everything would be all right. Lucy had said it numerous times, but when all hell is breaking loose around you, it is hard to listen to the voice of calm. The voice of panic sets in. You feel like just kicking and screaming which of course, can drown you just as fast as doing nothing. Doing too much or fighting too hard takes an enormous amount of energy. On the other hand, floating only gets you where you're going if the water is moving in the right direction, not to mention it takes a long time to reach your destination. But what happens when you listen to the voice of calm and take life one day at a time, giving it your best each day?

The third week of my temping experience was a good week. I did not work at all! Well, let me rephrase that. I was able to play catch up on my company's work. In the process I was able to get some marketing out and reorganize some things. Keisha popped up out of nowhere in the middle of the week.

Keisha: *Girl, what you going to do now? Next week you are not going to have a paycheck.*

Don't you find it interesting that the same little voice that told you it was embarrassing or humiliating is the same voice that sends you into panic when you aren't able to pay the bills? The voice of panic likes confusion and doesn't care what the situation is. However, the voice of calm will find hope in every situation:

Lucy: Veraunda, trust me, you are going to be fine. One day real soon, finances will not be a problem. Until then, do the best you can and NEVER discount your work. Each day you send out marketing material, make phone calls or invest time in EHAP Inc., you are planting a seed. Seeds are usually buried with dirt. If you try to watch it grow, it will seem like forever. But if you nurture the seed instead of dwelling on the growth process, before you know it there will be visual results of your labor. The season of harvest is coming; the waiting period is only temporary!

Lucy was absolutely right. I kept working at home. On Friday of that week, I got a surprise phone call. A youth group of almost two hundred were coming to Orlando for a retreat. They needed a speaker on very short notice. Someone who had heard me speak almost a year ago had recommended me. (A seed had been planted without me even knowing what the harvest would be or when the harvest would come.) They were going to pay me my asking price in cash onsite!

Perhaps you are in a situation you really don't want to be. Maybe it is a job you are not happy with. Maybe you are in school trying to better yourself and the work just seems overwhelming. You have to remind yourself it is only temporary. You are going *through* one situation to get to a better place. Don't dwell on where you are now, instead focus on where you are going. Think about the positives and if necessary, write them down on a piece of paper or in a journal. This will help you stay on task and keep your spirits up. You can't give up! You can't get bogged down in a pity party for yourself. Success is something that is achieved only when you push through to your dreams! Remember...well, let's let Lucy tell you. (Smile)

Lucy: My friend, it really is only temporary!

I was able to pay several bills with the "unexpected harvest" from speaking. The temping agency called me on Friday to give me my next assignment. It started out as a one-day fill-in for a receptionist at a local children's agency. I arrived about fifteen minutes early and just sat in the lobby. Keisha was trying to talk to me, but I refused to listen. When the supervisor arrived, she showed me my workstation. It was a nice reception area. My work assignment came as a surprise. "All we want you to do is answer the phones. There is not a lot of telephone or walk-in traffic, so if you have something you want to work on, feel free." WHAT??? Did I hear her correctly? I am going to get paid to do my own work as long as I answer the phones when they ring? Now this was cool! Then came the big extra. "Feel free to use the computer or the Internet. Some people get a little bored sitting up here." Well, she wouldn't have to worry about me getting bored! It was better than imaging all day!

It was the perfect temporary job! I could check my e-mails, send e-mails, and work on projects while getting paid for it! The first day I wrote half of this chapter. I was convinced I had hit gold. Keisha wasn't saying a word now! Wait, it gets better. Remember I said it was only a day assignment. Well, mid-morning, I received a phone call from the permanent receptionist. She was just calling to check on me. After telling her I was fine and appreciated the call, she said, "Oh, by the way, I am going to be transferring to another location. The position is going to be open if you are interested." She suggested I talk with the supervisor about the position. WOW! Now Lucy is talking and Keisha is quiet as a church mouse. (Well, almost).

Lucy: Veraunda, isn't this a blessing? If you can temp here for a couple of weeks, guess how much you can get accomplished. You can work on the book, work on some business proposals, keep up with your e-mails, phone calls, not to mention the pay is more than the government agency. This would be perfect!

Remember, I said Keisha was almost as quiet as a church mouse. She had to get her pessimistic two cents worth in.

Keisha: Well, Lucy has a point, but you start conducting the government stress management workshops in July. The contract is for the entire month of July which is only one week away. How are you gonna work that? You are only available three days a week.

Lucy: Veraunda, it is a possibility. Talk to the supervisor. Don't make any assumptions. Let's see what happens. You don't have anything to lose by asking.

I followed Lucy's voice of calm and reason. Guess what happened? I told the supervisor I was not interested in the full-time position because I had my own company. However, I would love to help the agency out by temping three days a week until they found someone. She immediately asked me about the following week. I was available all but one day; she said she would love to have me when I was available. I quickly typed up my availability, then called the temp agency to see if they would allow me to work three days a week. The temp agency told me it was up to the employer. I was in! What a miracle! I had a nice-sized contract with the county to do ten stress management seminars two days a week for a month. But I would not get paid for them until the following month. The children's agency would provide a steady paycheck in the meantime!

I'm here to tell you, if you just persevere through the storm, life will answer your call for help! Wait, the story has still another twist. When I started the second week at the children's agency, a woman that looked very familiar to me walked in the door. I cheated by looking at her nametag and saw she was the Vice-President of my former credit union. We started chatting, and the next thing I know we are talking about why I am no longer with the credit union. I explained I had left the State Attorney's Office to pursue my dream of speaking. Her face lit up. "What topics do you speak on?" I told her the array of topics. Immediately she responded, "Oh my gosh, we are looking for speakers for a conference I am working on in October! Do you have any information with you?" Well, of course I did. Lucy was just beaming by the time the lady left.

Lucy: See how life works itself out. Every day you walk on this earth is a day you should expect great things! If you had quit after the first week of temping, you would have missed this opportunity. You have to be convinced that not one day of your existence is in vain! When the storm hits, just keep looking for the sunshine to come. The lessons in the storm are invaluable and will last you a lifetime. Can you see the sun peaking from behind the clouds now? The storm really is only temporary!

This time Keisha really didn't have a word to say! But I can tell you my spirit was reflecting on the last four weeks. What started out as a dreaded mission to pay the bills had become an opportunity to network. Most importantly, I was receiving a steady income.

If you can't find the strength to dream through the storm, then work through it. I will admit my outlook on temping was very ugly when I started, but I knew I had to pay the bills. As hard as it was for me to go to the interview, I knew I had to do it. I did not have a lot of options. Sink or swim. Floating wasn't going to get me anywhere. I had been floating for almost four months. I didn't like the direction I was swimming, but I sure wasn't going to risk sinking.

Case in point, during my third week of temping I watched a television story about a woman who had been married to a very wealthy man. When they got a divorce, she agreed to quite a nice settlement. She had a luxury apartment in New York. She was a social butterfly while she was married, attending fundraisers, art shows and celebrity functions. Her background was in public relations. After the divorce she decided she was going to start her own company. The income was not enough to pay her bills. A few years after the divorce she found herself sinking in financial trouble. However, she continued to live as if nothing was changing. She floated on loans from friends. Before she knew it, the wind seeped out of the floatation device. She had borrowed over one hundred thousand dollars!

She was totally lost. The eviction notice seemed to stun her but not enough to get a job and work through the storm. As I watched the story, I kept saying how could she just sit there? The interviewer asked her why she didn't seek employment. Her answer was one that Keisha would give. She said she wanted to see her company make it and working outside of her home would not allow her to devote time to building the company. In essence, it was all or nothing. With that attitude, you probably won't be surprised at the outcome. The woman ended up living in homeless shelters. She went from riches to rags because she gave up during the storm.

I was outraged when they closed the story by saying she was taking her ex-husband to court to seek more money because he had become a millionaire since the divorce. Her premise was she should not have to suffer while he lived the good life with his new wife. Well, instead of letting the divorce sucker punch him, he kept working and rebuilt his wealth. She on the other hand, got comfortable with a six-figure settlement and floated through years of her life. When the winds of trouble started blowing, she did not respond, instead she expected them to just blow over. Boy, did they blow! They blew her right into poverty!

In her defense, she did try a couple of jobs, but she walked off within three months each time, citing depression and public humiliation as the reasons she just could not work in "any" environment. She had a voice like Keisha drowning her with a negative mentality. Here was an ivy-league, college-educated woman. No doubt, a woman with many corporate connections. (Anyone who can borrow a hundred thousand dollars from their friends has to be well connected). The interviewer didn't understand and neither did I. Where was her voice of calm and reason? Where was her desire to swim? A few nights in a homeless shelter would have done it for me. But for many people, they would rather drown in sorrow than find the energy to swim through the storms.

I know firsthand that swimming in a storm is extremely difficult. It is so easy to blame others for your storm. I've done it. But whose fault it is doesn't really matter in the long run. Survival is all that matters when it's over.

I made up my mind when I left the State Attorney's Office that I would not drown. End of discussion. I did not anticipate how rough the storm would get; after all, I was talented and educated. I certainly did not anticipate the emotional conflict the storm would cause. I had believed in myself since I was a little girl. When the financial storm came, it seemed to knock me off balance, but only for a moment. I had to refocus my energy on the possibilities. I had to remind myself that anything worth having is worth working for. No matter what Keisha said, I was still a woman with a vision! The dream had not vanished, instead it was being developed. Storms are always a part of having a dream. That is why so many people are not successful. They abandon the dream when hard times hit.

Temping provided me with some unique experiences. I gained a tremendous amount of knowledge from my various assignments. I learned how to operate a switchboard. But I also learned which telephone systems worked best, so when the time comes to purchase one for my company, I can be an informed consumer. I worked in a large purchasing department. I learned how large companies process bids and how to properly move purchase orders and invoices through the system.

My first temping assignment was as a receptionist for a homebuilder. It was interesting to find out how home warranties work, how contractors get paid and how many companies are used to build one house. I even worked for one company that had in-house computer technicians. I spoke with them about a problem I was having with my laptop. They tested it then repaired it for free! And the biggest reward was the ability to write parts of this book without interruption on several assignments.

The lesson is very simple; you can learn something new in every situation! The possibilities are endless when you walk into what seems like a whirlwind. I will be the first to admit, it will be scary! Use the anxiety to fuel your curiosity. What can the storm teach you? How will it make you a better person?

It was very clear by the third temping assignment. My experience was going to be a chapter in this book. I knew it would be encouraging to others to know I had to suck up my pride and go back to the basics of money management. Need money? Get a job. (Or in my case, get another job). I wasn't struggling alone. I was struggling just like everybody else does when they are starting out.

When I think about my various degrees of education, each new level of school was a struggle. Remember how excited you were when you were going to high school? You were getting closer to being independent. Do you remember how the first few weeks were always the hardest? With the promotion to the next grade or level, there is always a new school, new teachers and new friends. Although I was always excited about the promotion, I was usually terrified the first day of school.

College was no different. I experienced the same feelings all over again. I was glad I had made it to college, but I was scared to death of being away from home. I knew I would be all right; after all thousands of students arrived on campus each year and made it through. Entering a new environment is a challenge. Although I went to Florida State University for undergraduate and law school, the first couple of weeks in law school were just as scary as my first few weeks as a seventeen-year-old freshman. I was in the same city, on the same campus, but in a different environment with new challenges. From elementary to law school I struggled in the beginning, but each time life balanced out and the storm passed over. When the winds calmed down, when the rain stopped, and the sun started to emerge from behind the clouds, my path was clear again. Remember the voice of panic is always going to show up at the first sign of turbulence. Don't let the voice of panic pressure you into settling. Instead, listen to the voice of calm. The situation is only temporary.

Starting a company or changing directions to follow your dream is just like starting at a new school. You will be scared the first few weeks, but as you learn your way around, you will gain momentum. Almost every school has a mentor program to help you adjust to the new environment. Implement this idea into your life. Use other survival stories to empower you through your struggle. Align yourself with other people who have done what you are trying to do. Let them guide you through the process. Be honest with them about your fears and concerns. I had several speaking and author mentors who encouraged me through the storms. We shared ideas and networked. Each one of them had endured a storm, and each one reassured me that my struggle was only temporary.

I have continued to temp for a couple of reasons. Even when the skies are clear and the sun is shining, I still have debt. I have also learned a very valuable lesson about my spending habits. I don't **need** everything I want. Instead, I am learning to prioritize my spending while making sure I save for rainy days. I don't ever want to be so financially desperate again. However, I am thankful for the experience. I received a much-needed awakening. Prior to the financial storm, I had taken a lot for granted.

I made a deliberate decision to continue to temp when time permitted to generate extra income to pay off my bills. I am working very hard to be debt independent within three years. This means I want to pay for everything I want or need at the time of purchase. I am also learning a great deal about owning and operating a business. Now that my perspective has been refocused, the picture is clear: I will only be temping...*temporarily!*

Keisha: Guess what happened as soon as Veraunda finished writing this chapter! Oooh, you will never guess!

Lucy: Oh, no you don't! Let Veraunda tell her own story.

OK, since the voices are fighting about how this chapter will end, I will tell you Keisha is right. You would never guess what happened as soon as I thought I had finished this chapter.

I finished writing this chapter on Friday, September 29, 2001 while I was temping on a three-day assignment. That evening I was offered an unbelievable opportunity. A new entity was moving to Orlando. The entity was in its start-up stage and had numerous positions to fill. I had not really considered a position with the entity. First, I thought I did not want a full- time job. I had been offered several full-time positions since I started EHAP Inc. I had turned each one down without a second thought. Money or no money, I was on a mission and I had to see the dream through. I believed taking a full-time position would restrict me and my vision. Running a company is hard enough, but running a company and traveling is a double whammy! So full-time employment was not an option. As Keisha had pointed out many times: If I was going to work full-time, I might as well go back to practicing law. Simply put, I didn't want to do it! Keisha reminded me that a part time position would be almost impossible to get.

Keisha: Girl, here you go again with these visions of grandeur and how life should just come together for you. What are you going to do at a governmental entity part time? Oh, I get it. You are going to answer phones. When are you going to get enough of this foolishness? You are a LAWYER. Why don't you become a professor if you want to be in higher education. This dream of yours is getting ridiculous!

Lucy: Veraunda, life is full of possibilities. You don't know what is available at the entity. Talk with the administrators and see what they have for you.

My second area of concern was a history issue. I had a connection with a rival entity. The entity basically stole the viability of this entity years ago. I really didn't know how great my chances were of landing a job at the newly revived entity.

70

Despite the concerns and Keisha's constant negativity, I took Lucy's advice. I offered my services to the administration. I started with offering to help in anyway I could. I knew the skeleton start-up crew were all new to Orlando, and this entity was going to be an historic undertaking. It's an entity with a tradition of excellence. The entity was a result of over twenty years of controversy and debate. It was long overdue. The office at the time of my volunteering to help consisted of three administrators and an executive assistant.

I literally volunteered to help anywhere they needed it. Let me be clear about this, I offered to help without pay. I would help answer phones or set up files, or any task that needed to be done. I just wanted to be a blessing to those who were charting new territory. When I made the offer, I was very serious. Keisha thought I was out of my mind!

Keisha: Oh no, you didn't! Girl, what is wrong with you? Are you crazy? We have no money, we are struggling and you volunteer to help do whatever for no compensation! You are really starting to concern me. You can't afford to do anything for free right now. You better hope they don't take you up on your offer because we are not working for free! Temping is bad enough as it is, but temping is better than working for free!

Lucy: Veraunda, we are going to help if they call. It is better to give than to receive, and you know as well as I do, you are going to be just fine. You have not lost anything up to this point, and you aren't going to lose anything now. You did the right thing by volunteering your assistance.

The administrators told me they just might take me up on my offer. I started joking about what I could do. I even threw out an hourly wage I would settle for. It was just a few dollars more than I was making temping. The joke became serious when the administrators considered my offer. That Friday evening I was offered a part-time professional position. I was so excited and thankful I could have kissed everyone in the office! Here is the kicker, they were going to pay me as a professional. I was also going to have the flexibility I needed to continue to run EHAP, Inc.! See, you really don't have to settle!

This position was going to pay me well and allow me to follow my dreams!

My temping was over after just four assignments. Once I had resolved that everything was going to be all right, my circumstances improved dramatically. I am a firm believer my financial storm was a test of my endurance. What was I willing to do to make my dream a reality? How would I react when the storm hit? Would I run? Would I give up? Would I become depressed and stop believing in my dream?

I thought I had finished this chapter after this paragraph. I was getting ready to ship it off to my editors for proofing. I was rejoicing in my great job! Problem solved! Whew, the storm was over! Life will send you reminders that surviving is a continuous process. The next phase was determining how I would respond in the presence of my enemies!

In all honesty, it was a difficult time. Keisha constantly nagged at me and tried to discourage me from continuing with my dream. I had moments that I wanted to give up, but I knew I couldn't. I kept my faith strong and often thought about my possibilities. When the storm was over, I knew the success would be worth the struggle. You have to be sure of the same.

When your storm hits, what are you going to do? Float, sink or swim? Which voice are you going to listen to? The voice of panic or the voice of calm? If you are in the middle of your storm, are you giving up, or are you fighting with everything in you to make it through the rough times? I am telling you, no matter what the storm, don't give up! Start swimming and watch the storm start to lessen in intensity. Worst-case scenario, make up some names for the voices that are tugging at you and have some fun. I promised Lucy she could have the last word in this chapter.

Lucy: Dear friend, please know that no matter what your storm is at the moment, not only can you get through it, YOU WILL GET THROUGH IT! It really is only temporary!

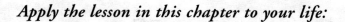

Apply the lesson in this chapter to your life:

What situation in your life is causing you to question your direction?

What emotional and physical outlets can you utilize to ease the difficulty until you conquer the challenge?

You Don't Have To Settle!

In the presence of my enemies!

After three months in the organization or "on the job", the same person who brought me in changed my classification and lowered my pay by ten dollars an hour. Our relationship had started to change slowly but surely. I started looking for the good in the situation. I sent her a letter thanking her for helping me get me in the door. I was also thankful because as a result of her friendship I had experienced twelve years of blessings. This person was one of my dearest friends. Not only was the relationship changing, she actively started campaigning against me. Her coworkers found this behavior odd. When they were rallying for me, she was rallying against me. One director was adamant about trying to keep me in her department. My "friend" was her immediate supervisor. My "friend" flat out told the director she couldn't hire me. In plain English, my "friend" no longer wanted me in the organization. My "friend" had become my enemy. There are tests along our journey. I took the position at least I still had a job and it was paying more than what I had made temping. It was also flexible which allowed me to continue speaking and traveling. Now how long I would be there was an unknown variable. So I chose to be thankful for each day I worked.   Keisha on the other hand could not believe it.

Keisha: Oh no she didn't bring you in here, then just act like you weren't a valuable part of this process! Doesn't she know you have done your work? Doesn't she know you believe in this organization and vision? Doesn't she know who you are? Doesn't she know you are going to be wealthy and would pay off all of her debt? Doesn't she know you would gladly write this organization a huge check to help others live their dreams? What is she doing and why? Doesn't she know you need the money right now? Doesn't she know you are barely making it? How could she feel good about what she is doing? It's ok! Just like you tell the kids in your speaking engagements you can show her better than you can tell her!

This wasn't the time for Lucy to respond! Very simply, this person knew what my situation was. She was the angel God used to bail me out of my financial troubles temporarily. So the question wasn't, did she know? The question was, did she care? I had to see it from a different perspective in order to make it through each day. Something I had done had caused her to reevaluate our relationship. Our relationship was no different than the gangs. As long as I was abiding by her life laws and doing everything she wanted, I was safe. When those laws were questioned or violated, I was subject to whatever punishment she felt was fair. In this case it started out with a reduction in pay. The next phase of punishment was crushing.

My mother was diagnosed with stomach cancer in February of 2002. My enemy gave her apologies. She told me to be there for my mother. She also told me to let her know what she could do. Words are easy to say, backing them up shows who you really are and if you really care.

It was a well-developed plan. Under the guise of, "The need for your services is decreasing as we hire other employees." They put the plan into action. The second phase started shortly after I wrote an email to my "friend" asking her what the nature of the problem was. In March, as our relationship continued to deteriorate, I wrote to her asking for dialogue about whatever was bothering her while apologizing for whatever I may have done to contribute to the situation. I also thanked her for her friendship over the years. It was important to me to acknowledge the good in spite of the current state of our relationship.

Instead of a discussion about the relationship I was pulled into an office and told my time was drawing near. "Thank you for your help, but we aren't going to need you much longer." No date was given. The meeting was closed by a reminder by my "friend" this job was only temporary. It is funny I had already written a chapter for this book entitled "It's only temporary." The words from that chapter were coming back to hit me full force. Our visions have a voice. The question is, are we going to listen to the voice when it speaks? In this case, I thought this job was a perfect compliment to my vision. It should have been a win-win situation for all parties involved.

As time passed, I was sure professionalism would govern our interactions and I would be given at least a two week-notice prior to my contract expiring to seek other options for employment. Even the most heartless person would not just leave someone out in the cold. Or maybe they would if they were staying up at night thinking about how to hurt you and cause you pain. My "enemy" and her accomplice never told me the date my employment would end. I went in the office on a Friday in May. I worked my scheduled hours and left. As I was driving home, my cell phone rang. It was the accomplice saying she needed me to fax my timesheet because my contract had expired. I could hear the satisfaction in her voice. Their plan had worked. They had won, I was gone! The leader of the organization was away on business and I had no recourse. What a perfect execution!

During your journey you will always have good versus evil. In my case I believe the evil started as a result of jealousy and intimidation. Please keep in mind this is my opinion. The only thing I could do is guess as to what really happened because to this day there hasn't been any conversation about the relationship. What was said by others helped me reach my opinion. Even after I was gone, the plot continued. Others tried to hire me in their department. Because my "friend" was so far up the ladder most of the hiring had to be approved by her. She denied the requests on several occasions and became very adamant when people attempted to find out why they couldn't hire me.

On other occasions when positions were discussed and my name came up, she would bring up my weaknesses to try to discourage the individuals from considering me. On one occasion she lied by telling the interested individuals I had no interest in a full-time job. That was not true. What was true, was I did not want a job that prohibited me from making my vision a reality. So her efforts to "get rid of me" worked. For two months as my mom was fighting for her life. I was fighting for mine as well. I was temping at odd jobs trying to keep from drowning in my debt. I was angry about my plight, but also extremely concerned about how to be there for my mother when I had to work. Far in the background was my vision.

Now, as I write this I have a smile on my face because there are going to be people who *think* they are hurting you, when the truth is they are only making you stronger. Lucy stepped in immediately.

Lucy: Veraunda, be thankful for the 12 years of friendship. Be thankful for all of the blessings she brought into your life when you needed them. This is a new time and perhaps her season has passed.

Keisha: Perhaps her season has passed???? Lucy you are crazy! Her season is definitely up! Your mother is battling cancer. You don't have a job because your so-called friend turned enemy just screwed you out of a job! Now what are you going to do? I say what I said a year ago we should go back to being a lawyer. You don't have to put up with this crap! Your enemy isn't worth a thank you! Friends don't screw friends! She just undermined all of the good work she did in those twelve years. Hell, it would be one thing if she wasn't helping you, but purposely trying to hurt you is just evil!

Lucy: Veraunda, don't listen to her! If the friendship is over and the job is over that is fine. But your dream is not over! People will disappoint you, but your dream has nothing to do with anyone other than you. It's not for them to care about you and your survival. This is YOUR dream and nobody will ever care as much about you as you will. Veraunda, you have made it through the past two and a half years, why on earth would you give up just because your contract expired? Don't be fooled, the situation is still a temporary one.

Lucy had an excellent point. My dream had nothing to do with a contract expiring or with an enemy screwing me out of a job. I sucked up my anger and redirected my energy. My mother was in and out of the hospital. The bills were backing up again, I was speaking some but once again my expenses were more than my income. My heart was heavy.

My spirit finally broke on Monday, June 12, 2002. The doctors said there was nothing else they could do for my mother. Here I was with no real job, bills stacking up, and my mother was dying. What do you do when everything seems to be out of sync? What do you do when the whole world seems to be crushing in from all sides? Financial struggles were one thing, but now I was forced to deal with the possibility of losing my mother. The voices in my head started to multiply. I felt angry that during one of the most difficult losses a child can experience, I had to struggle financially because of an enemy. I felt overwhelmed because I had to go temp each day then rush over to the hospital in the evenings to spend time with my mother. I felt alone. I thought at least if I had still been with the State Attorney's Office I would have vacation time to take off without worrying about money. I would be able to spend each day with my mom. This season of my life was horrible! I was overwhelmed, I was tired and I was scared!

The bill collectors were calling. I would try to explain my situation to them. They didn't care. One customer service representative told me I needed to sell my car or trade it in for something I could afford. I couldn't believe it! I told her I was not going to lose my car. I also told her I was in a temporary period of struggle. With an attitude she told me I should try borrowing the money. Keisha couldn't help herself:

Keisha: *Borrow the money from who? Oh, my God! It doesn't get any worse than this! Your mother is dying, the bill collectors are calling, what are you going to do? I believe in our dream, but right now, the dream isn't paying the bills. I'm not saying give up, I am saying go back to where you know you are wanted. Go back to where you know you are good. You are an outstanding prosecutor. You don't have to struggle like this. This is self-torture! I don't see how it's going to get any better if you don't go back to practicing law.*

Lucy: *Veraunda, you are a person of faith. Just stand still and know there is a God. He is faithful! This is a temporary situation!*

Keisha: *Girl, shut up! Her mother is dying and she has no real job! What on earth are you talking about, you must be blind if you don't see she is about to lose everything. Just shut up! Veraunda listen to me, get through your mother's illness and then go get a real job! You don't have to depend on a contract or a temping assignment to make it. You had real job security and full benefits when you worked for the government. People are crazy and this is crazy! How could you put yourself in a position like this? You see what happens when you trust people? They screw you! They don't care what happens to you, they don't care that your mother is in the hospital. It is really simple, if they cared they wouldn't have acted in the manner they did. So screw them right back!*

Lucy tried her best to keep me calm. Yes, when I took the position with the organization, I knew it was a temporary position. But with time and the steady pay checks, I got comfortable. I thought it would work out until I was on my feet. I thought this was the answer to ease my financial problems. Surely the position would have lasted until my company was a little more stable or I had the opportunity to pay off some of my debt. No matter what I thought, things weren't looking good for me. My friend had turned into my enemy. She was after me and my job with a vengeance I had not experienced in my seventeen years of working. I felt her wrath in every area of my life. I was so angry with her! Lucy reminded me it was not about her.

Lucy: *Veraunda, you cannot take this personally! This is not about you! Her evilness can't hurt you unless you allow it to. Remember the philosopher Epictetus said, "It's not what happens to you, but how you react to it that matters." Don't you dare let her issues become your issues. Hold your head up, do what you need to do to get beyond this challenge. Your victory is the best remedy for her evilness. Remember you have a vision! Your vision is bigger than anything she has ever seen for herself. Think about this. You are coming into this organization smiling, making friends. Your light might expose her areas of darkness. You are a powerful young lady. Darkness is afraid of the light, Veraunda.*

Keisha: I am not disagreeing with Lucy on this point. I am simply saying, you have worked with her before. You have had twelve years of friendship which included divorces, marriages, and surgeries. You have been a good friend to her!

Lucy: And she has been a good friend to you! Don't forget that Veraunda!

Keisha: Did I interrupt you? No! So let me finish! Veraunda, it's not about the past. It is about here and now. She has turned on you. Clearly, you are no longer her friend. So the question becomes now that she is intentionally going after you are you going to just stand by and let her destroy your life?

Lucy: Veraunda that is super dramatic! Keisha has forgotten, your destiny has already been predetermined by a power much higher than your ex-friend! No weapon formed against you shall prosper! No person can keep you from the greatness of your destiny. Look at it this way. It is sad she has chosen to cut herself off from your light and prosperity. But you will be victorious despite your enemies.

Keisha: Wow, that's a pretty bold and cocky statement!

Lucy: No, it is a truthful statement. Veraunda, where you are going, very few people can go with you. Along the journey up the mountain you will lose friends and make plenty of enemies. You are doing what they don't have the courage to do. Your boldness, your vision, your refusal to settle will not be accepted by everyone. It is a price of being who you are. Remember, when you gave a speech for the investiture of some local judges? You told them the African American writer, Lorraine Hansberry said, "The thing that makes you exceptional, is inevitably the thing that must also make you lonely." Just like it applied to the judges it applies to you! Your light is so bright that for those who are comfortable settling, they want to blow your light out, steal the batteries or pull the plug to your source. But it's not that easy unless you let them dim your light. Keep shining, Veraunda!

Keisha: *Yes, your light is bright, but your bills are due, including the electricity bill, so I hope you can shine some light on your finances.*

Thursday June 15th, my temping assignment was filing some papers for a huge company. I thought I was going to lose my mind. Keisha was trying to talk to me and push me to reapply at the State Attorney's Office. I loved my job as a prosecutor. I knew it would be rewarding in addition to paying the bills. However, now that I had seen the vision there was no way I could turn back. At lunch I drove to a local park to eat in my car. I just sat and cried out to God. "I need your help! You promised me you would take care of me! Why aren't you helping me???"

I called a friend who told me it was going to be ok. She talked me through the emotional low I was experiencing. She reminded me to stand firmly in my faith. I went back to work because I desperately needed the money. I was checking my messages constantly. My mother was on a day-by-day basis now. I was calling the hospital four times during the work day. Today, when I checked my messages there was a voice mail from my one of my mother's friends. Her voice was full of panic. "Veraunda, you better get down here fast, they have moved your mother. I called the hospital immediately. The nurse told me my mother was ok. She was stable and had been moved to the Cancer Critical Care unit. She was resting, the move was a lateral move. I was relieved but my heart was heavy.

Keisha: *Veraunda, you can't take anymore!*

Lucy: *Oh, yes you can! God won't put more on you than you can bear! Be strong! Be encouraged!*

Keisha: *Don't be foolish! This is absolutely the worst situation to be in. You are hurting, you are scared, you are struggling and you can't keep pursuing this dream right now. What about your mother? Put everything on hold. You aren't abandoning the dream. It's o.k. Lucy keeps saying it is only temporary, so this is just a short leave of absence. If you don't put* *the dream on hold, your entire world is going to cave in! You have got to survive. Go ahead and apply for a full-time job.*

Lucy: *She is absolutely right about one thing, you must survive in the presence of your enemies and in the face of adversity. We have traveled this road before. The obstacles have changed a little, but you have the strength to survive them!*

My mother passed in June on Fathers Day, 2002. I still had no job, and I knew I had to go to work. Whitehall Staffing was doing everything they could to keep me working. They knew I was barely making it. The temp agency had me come work with them the Friday before my mother's death. The Monday following my mother's death I was assigned to the American Cancer Society (ACS). This was a true miracle in what appeared to be a monster of an emotional mess.

When I arrived at the American Cancer Society I was greeted by an older woman who was the receptionist. She was a Christian lady with a sweet spirit. She explained she was going to have hip replacement surgery and would be out for quite some time. Perhaps if I was interested they could bring me back to cover for her. I tell you some stability in my life right now would be great!

I sat in the waiting area and started reading some of the literature on cancer. It is amazing, not once during my mother's illness did I do any independent research on cancer. I knew about the American Cancer Society but I didn't know they had so many support programs for patients and their families. When I met the supervisor, I immediately told her about my mother's passing. I also said I didn't think it was a coincidence I was assigned to the Cancer Society. She shared with me she had lost a loved one to cancer prior to working for ACS. We both were crying as we shared our stories. She couldn't believe I was working on the day after my mother's death. First, I had no choice financially. Second, I needed to stay busy.

ACS was a bright place to work. The atmosphere was free-spirited but very productive. Everyone introduced themselves to me. I was given an office to work in. My assignment was a simple one. They wanted me to create a database for some labels. No problem. This was a one-day, possibly two-day assignment. By midday, the supervisor asked me if I could come back tomorrow. They had plenty of work and if I would like to stay, they would love to have me. I was thankful!

On Tuesday morning when I reported to work, I was blessed by two young interns. The first intern was the daughter of one of my former judges. During the summer college break she was interning with ACS. Her mom was a breast cancer survivor. She talked about the process and how difficult it was for her family. Her story had a happy ending. Her mother completed treatment successfully and was doing well.

The second intern had a different story. She was in college and interning with ACS just like the first young lady. Her mother had also been diagnosed with cancer. Her mother like mine did not survive. She was sixteen years old when her mother passed. She shared with me how difficult it was to be a teenager without her mother. She said her dad had done a wonderful job raising her alone, but nothing can replace your mother. She reflected on how difficult dating was because her mother wasn't there to meet her boyfriends. She remembered crying at her High School graduation because her mother wasn't present. She also talked about the anxiety she faces when there are major events in her life because she misses her mother's presence as she is achieving her dreams or experiencing life's challenges. She closed by saying, "Veraunda, be thankful you had your mother for your proms, high school graduation, your college graduation, your wedding, your law school graduation and even the publishing of your first book. You had your mother for thirty- two years. I only had mine for sixteen."

I was in deep thought now. What this twenty-year-old young lady had shared with me was powerful! Our conversation had given me a new perspective not only on my mother's life, but on my enemies.

Lucy: Veraunda, life is amazing isn't it. Think about where you are at this very moment. You are working in an organization which dedicates all of its resources to the battle against cancer. You are in an environment where every person here is supporting you during this difficult time.

Many of the employees have had a personal experience with losing a loved one to cancer. You are not alone on this journey.

If you had been working for the other organization you would be surrounded by all of the foolishness your enemies continually kept plotting. Here, you are at peace. No evil looks, no ignoring you, no plotting against you. God has removed you from the presence of your enemies and placed you in a supportive group of allies. Doesn't it feel good not having to fight for a change?

Keisha: *Yes, it does feel good not to have to fight with people who don't like you for whatever reason. I also agree with Lucy this is a good environment for you right now. I hate to bring you back to reality for a few moments, but I must remind you as Lucy has been telling you all along, this is only temporary. So don't get too comfortable here. Instead just hope this assignment lasts all week.*

I didn't have the energy to agree with Keisha or give her reality check much thought. I was literally taking it day by day. My family was making the arrangements for my mother's home going service. I was glad to be working for ACS. I learned more about cancer in two days than I had in four months of my mother's battle with the deadly disease. On Wednesday, I sent out an email entitled, "What if tomorrow never comes?" The email was my "Thought that makes a difference" for June. I received hundreds of emails offering condolences and prayers. I included the funeral information for those who wanted to attend, I also asked for donations to the ACS in my mother's honor instead of flowers.

Your enemies will appear when you least expect them. A former coworker received the email and passed the news to my enemy. My cell phone rang and guess who was on the other line? You got it, the enemy pretending to care! My spirit was instantly stirred! The conversation was short but enough to shake me up:

Enemy: *Hello Veraunda, this is _____.*

Keisha: *We know who it is! How dare she call us!*

Enemy: I am so sorry to hear about your mother.

Keisha: She is a lying bitch! How dare she! Hang up Veraunda!

Lucy: Keisha, watch your mouth!

Keisha: I'm just keeping it real! I don't have to be perfect! This woman has been straight out evil! Calling her a name is minimal compared to what she had done to us!

Lucy: Veraunda, be nice. Maybe this is the turning point for the two of you.

Keisha: Girl, I doubt it!

Enemy: Is there anything I can do?

Keisha: Not a damn thing!

Veraunda: No thank you.

Enemy: When is the service?

Keisha: None of her business! Ask her if she really cares? Ask her if she has been concerned the last month or so when you didn't have a job and she knew your mother was diagnosed with cancer! Ask her if she cared how you were paying your bills?

Lucy: Veraunda, don't you dare! It is not going to make a difference in this situation. She has shown you who she is believe her and move on.

Veraunda: The service is Friday.

Enemy: Oh, I wish I could come, but my son is graduating from boot camp in the Carolinas.

Keisha: Good! We don't want her evil spirit disturbing your mother's homegoing service anyway! What nerve she has!

Veraunda: No problem.

Enemy: You know I would be there if I could. What can I do?

Veraunda: Nothing, thank you.

Enemy: Well, you know I am here for you and I love you.

Keisha: WHAT??? Is she crazy! How can she form her lips to say she loves you when she just screwed you big time! Now your mother has died and she loves you! Give me a break!!! Curse her out Veraunda! She has hit the last nerve!

Lucy: Veraunda, think about this, you haven't had to call her for anything. She is calling you out of guilt. She knows better than anyone that she screwed you. You don't have to say one word about it. It was her plan. She executed it without a second thought, so instead of buying into Keisha's anger, why don't we just leave it where it is. God has already worked it out so you won't have to be in the presence of your enemies during the services. You have been put in a new environment of support and your bills are being paid.

Keisha: Barely!

Lucy: Nevertheless, you are fine without her! Her attempt to hurt you really hasn't been successful has it? You are doing ok. You are surviving despite your enemies. That is what you need to convey. Simply, you are fine and you don't need her! Your source is far greater than she could ever be. He will supply all of your needs. Rest in his comfort Veraunda. You are much bigger than your enemies which is part of the reason they hate you! Just bless her and move on.

Enemy: If there is anything I can do, please call me.

Veraunda: O.K. Thank you for calling.

Keisha: Thank you hell! The nerve of her!

Lucy: Just let it go. It was a kind gesture. Move on, you can't dwell on your enemies! But you sure can dwell in their presence.

I wish it would have been that simple. On Wednesday before the funeral, my door bell rang unexpectedly. Imagine my surprise when I looked through the wooden blinds and saw my enemy's husband at the door. I didn't see anyone else so I opened the door with as much calm as I could. I could feel my blood pressure rising. My face was hardening. As soon as I opened the door, here comes the enemy around the corner with a plant (a peace lily of all plants) and a card. I was finishing an emotional conversation with a friend and mentor about the loss of my mother. I was walking her to the door with a new sense of strength to make it through this process and up pops the enemy!

Keisha: Girl, don't you dare invite them in. Don't entertain them, just slam the door in their face. I told you this woman has no conscious at all!

Lucy: Veraunda, hear them out. I agree with Keisha, don't entertain them but do hear them out. Right now your strength is crucial to survive your mother's home going service. Stay focused.

You could tell the enemy and her husband were very uncomfortable in my presence:

Enemy: We just wanted to stop by and offer our condolences. How are you doing?

Veraunda: I am doing fine, I am getting ready to go to my grandmothers house. Thanks for stopping by.

We were standing in the door of my home just looking at each other. I had not bothered to invite them in. I was trying to minimize the conversation and the time I had to be in their presence. It didn't work. When my enemy handed me the plant,

I took it inside the house and invited them in for a moment. To make sure no one got the wrong picture I stood in the kitchen, making it clear I didn't want them to get comfortable.

Enemy: Is there anything we can do?

Veraunda: No, thank you. We have taken care of everything.

Enemy: Well, we are leaving tomorrow to go out of town, but if you need me call me.

Keisha: Tell her to hold her breath and see what happens! When you needed her she showed you her backside. So, thanks but no thanks!

Veraunda: Ok, I better get moving, my grandmother is expecting me.

As everyone is standing in the most awkward situation I have ever seen, the enemy comes over and gives me a hug. I felt my body tense up.

Lucy: Hug her back, let your light shine.

Keisha: Girl, all of this woman's darkness might extinguish your light!

I gave a weak hug back when she opened her mouth to speak words I know she didn't mean:

Enemy: You know I love you, right?

Keisha: Veraunda slap her right now! Maybe she will realize she is telling a bold face lie! Love doesn't hurt! Slap her Veraunda!

Lucy: Nope, stay calm, breathe and tell her you love her too.

Keisha: What? I swear, I am the only sane person here. Veraunda you have been ignoring me this entire time, but I tell you what! If you tell her you love her you will be lying just like she is! You don't love her. You HATE her! You hate what she did to you! You hate the fact she had the nerve to just show up unannounced to your house!

Lucy: *Yes, you hate what she has chosen to do in her capacity as an administrator to you. You hate she didn't have the courage to discuss the real issues with you. You don't appreciate her just popping up at your home. You hate your friendship has ended the way it did. But you don't hate her.*

Veraunda: *I love you too.*

I forced myself to say it. I wanted to get it over with and stop the voices in my head. The enemy's husband came over and gave me a hug as well. I hugged him back. After all, I didn't have any problems with him. I showed the enemy to the door. As soon as I closed the door, I turned to my mentor and said "Can you believe they had the audacity to show up at my door?" I pulled myself together and decided to regroup. My mentor advised me to take all of my energy and channel it towards getting through the wake and the service. She advised I was going to need all the strength I could find. She knew first hand, she had also lost her mother when she was thirty-two years old.

Let's fast forward a month to July of 2002. I had several job opportunities arising. I was concerned about taking a full-time job which would pull me away from my vision. Almost two months after my enemy screwed me out of the organization, I was rehired under a new contract and a new department. There is a beauty in dwelling in the presence of your enemies which can only be revealed with time and endurance.

A table will be prepared before you in their presence. Not only was I rehired, my salary and hours were increased in addition to my parking being paid for. This may sound simple, but the little things make a big difference. I was paying for parking when I worked for my enemy. She claimed she couldn't get parking for temporary employees. It is amazing how my Creator makes his point! He will make a way out of no way. The new position also afforded me the flexibility to keep traveling, writing and running EHAP, Inc.

Within two weeks of my return to work my enemy was rushed to the hospital for an anxiety attack. I kept working. One of the administrators knew we had been friends. He came down to tell me I should go with her to help answer questions for the paramedics. My spirit was at peace and very clear:

Lucy: The only thing you can do for your enemy right now is bless her with your prayers.

Keisha: I totally agree with Lucy this time. What goes around comes around. We aren't going to get involved with evil thoughts right now. Even I know your ability to wish her well is not about her, it is about your integrity. I would be remiss if I didn't remind you she hasn't called back to check on you not one time after her so-called "I love you and I am here for you" show. She barely speaks when you pass in the hall. We have been fine without her, now blessing her with prayer would really be the icing on the cake. She just walked away, you stand fast in your integrity.

Lucy: Wow, if Keisha is in agreement we know we are on the right track. Say a prayer and graciously decline the invitation to get involved.

I responded to the administrator accordingly by indicating she was surrounded by enough people who could help her, I would just be in the way. I would say a prayer. If they needed to ask me some questions, I would be happy to assist in anyway I could. Her husband was here and would be more than capable of providing what she needed. When the administrator left I said a short prayer:

Veraunda: Lord, I pray you bless my enemy, I pray for physical and emotional healing. Finally, if there is a way you would like to use me in this process I am open and willing. Amen.

I left it in my Creator's hands which of course were much more capable than I could ever be of making a positive impact in this situation. I did send a card wishing her a speedy recovery. I signed the card "Blessings, Veraunda" instead of the often misused word "Love." When she returned to work, I asked her how she was feeling. She said much better. In turn she asked me how I was doing. I was fine. Each time I see her I speak. I acknowledge her presence for a very simple reason: I want to be clear; I am dwelling in spite of her presence against me. I am standing firmly in my vision. I am confident in my destiny! As Maya Angelou proclaimed, "I shall not be moved!"

When you start to live your dreams, your enemies will pop up all over the place! You will start to experience people's evilness in ways you could not have imagined when you were just settling. Think about it, if you sit on the first floor looking at the staircase, it doesn't take any energy to ponder how many levels there are or where the staircase leads. But if you are serious about elevation in life, you must climb the stairs. Unfortunately, there is no escalator or elevator to your dreams. It is a hard and steady climb up one step at a time to the top. As a wise leader told me, "Don't waste your time trying to rationalize your enemy's behavior. It isn't going to make sense to you! Remember this isn't about you. You keep looking ahead and climbing up."

I am learning some tremendous lessons dwelling in the presence of my enemies. Instead of spending my time fighting them, I am being blessed by them. I have written three new speeches for corporate offices as a result of my experiences. This chapter is another result of their tactics. I have also gained some thicker skin to weather future storms. I am learning the importance of choosing your battles carefully. I am experiencing new depths of strength and endurance. I am privileged to see the behind-the-scenes action of office drama. I am turning it into a way to bless others dealing with the same mess. My enemies are training me for bigger and better things. I am learning how to stand still in the midst of adversity. I am gaining insight about relationships and how they change when power and individual agendas start playing a role. These are all skills I need to be an effective leader of my company. I believe I am being prepared for the next level of my journey.

I heard a pastor tell the Biblical story of David and Goliath. He put a very different spin on the story than I had heard in other sermons. He talked about how big Goliath was, how small and seemingly unprepared David was in comparison to the giant. It appeared David was a sure loser in this battle. David refused the armor that was offered to him, because it didn't fit him. He also had one small weapon, a sling shot. But, David had been preparing all along as a Shepherd to fight the giant. He just didn't know it. He had used a sling shot to kill many enemies. Every time an animal threatened his flock of sheep, he would slay them with a single rock.

The pastor's closing was powerful: "God doesn't intend for us to fight the battle, it has already been won. All He wants us to do is show up!"

Each month I send out inspirational messages to thousands of readers across the country via email. I close this chapter with the "Thought that makes a difference!" for the month of November 2002.

"In the presence of my enemies!"'

What do you do when you are surrounded by people who are attacking you or hoping you will fail? Over the last year I started asking for wisdom, strength, courage and the exposure of my enemies in my prayers. I have always known that everyone won't like me. That isn't a problem. The dilemma comes when the people who don't like you for whatever reason decide to actively try to block your success.

I knew people would talk about you. But, I couldn't imagine that adults would pray for you to get sick. I couldn't imagine that someone would, after 12 years of "friendship," decide to completely sabotage your career. This same "friend" showed up on my doorstep when my mother died, told me she loved me, then went right back to trying to hurt me in the professional arena. I couldn't imagine that a 52-year-old woman would start rumors that were absolutely not true. I couldn't imagine that people could be so evil. But all of these things have happened to me in the last six months. I started requesting wisdom and guidance about my enemies. On some days I wanted to walk away. But the question became, why would I let my enemy win? My spirit became very clear: Those who think they are fighting me are only making me stronger. This time is just a preparation course to get me ready *for the next level. Every major leader has had an enemy! I cannot run a multimillion dollar, international company if I don't know how to dwell in the presence of my enemies. I hope the following quotes and scriptures that came to my spirit bless you as much as they have blessed me. **How do you dwell in the presence of your enemies?** 1) Love your enemies, bless those who curse you, do good to those who hate you and pray for those who spitefully use you – Matthew 5:44 (It's hard…but it works!) 2) When people show you who they are, believe them! - Iylana Vanzant 3) Though an army may encamp against me, my heart shall not fear. – Psalm 27:3 4) To see your enemy and know him is a part of the complete education of man – Marcus Garvey 5) Remember your enemies will be made your footstool – Hebrews 10:13 6) Fret not thyself because of evildoers, nor be envious of the workers of iniquity for they shall soon be cut down like the grass! - Psalm 37:1-2 7) Pray for God to deliver you from the traps they have laid for you. Psalm 141:9 8) Become determined…"I shall not be moved!" Maya Angelou. Finally, be very clear…your Creator, if you are faith-based, has already promised you this…**He will make a table in the presence of your enemies!** (Psalm 23:5) The 27th Psalm: Verses 11-14 closes this "thought" perfectly: Teach me your way Lord, and lead me in a smooth path, because of my enemies. Do not deliver me to the will of my adversaries, for false witnesses have risen against me and they breathe out violence. I would have lost heart, unless I had believed that I would see the goodness of the Lord in the land of the living. Wait on the Lord. Be of good courage and He shall strengthen your heart; wait I say on the Lord!*

The drama has continued as enemies continue to trot into my path. There has been gossip, rumors, backstabbing, prayers against my presence, in addition to not speaking to me episodes. It has frustrated me, disappointed me and hurt me. The bottom line is I am still pursuing my dream in the presence of my enemies. I am determined, "I shall not be moved!" I am climbing up the mountain because I know the view will be spectacular from two angles: First, me looking around at the vastness of the territory I have traveled and enjoying the view from the top! Second, I will be looking down at those who were afraid to follow their own dreams looking up at me wondering, "How did *she* get there?" The secret is quite simple, while they chose to spend their energy, fighting me, envying me, talking about me and hating me, I chose to spend my energy climbing above their pettiness, jealousy and fears. In short, I kept moving forward in spite of the presence of my enemies.

You will encounter the same thing on your journey. Forces will come against you full speed when you make a decision to live your dream. People will start turning on you when you need them the most. Your courage and your light will expose their darkness. It's sick, but often your enemy is praying for your failure so they can win. The question becomes what are they winning? If you fail, they have the pleasure of saying I told you so and continuing the gossip. We have seen this cycle many times in our life. People enjoy watching your pain and misery because it takes the focus off of their own miserable lives. In plain English: when you are excelling, it reminds them that they are settling!

Your enemies are fighting you to survive in their own dark world. It is sad and unfortunate, but it is the truth. Once you realize they are settling, it makes it easier for you to leave them where they are and move forward with your dream. Think about this. Have you ever heard them talk about their vision? Have they ever pushed past their fears to achieve anything? My guess is probably not. When I think about my enemy, she has talked about writing a book. The book was about people and how they play games. She has never gotten past talking about it. So here she is playing games and settling. While she is living her book, I am writing mine.

If you are pursuing your dream, I can promise you the attacks will come from all sides. Your finances, your family and your friends will all present challenges at some point during your journey. Your faith is the biggest challenge of all. Don't let your enemies' attacks divert your attention. Don't let the attack rob you of your faith. You keep pursuing in the presence of your enemies. Make up your mind, you shall not be moved! Keep climbing, keep pushing, keep moving forward! Remember you don't have to fight the battle, all you have to do is show up! Your Creator has already prepared a table for you in the presence of your enemies!

Apply the lesson in this chapter in your life:

Who are the enemies in your life?

How can you continue to be a bright light in a dark environment despite the challenges presented by your enemies?

I assure you, your vision will be so big it will scare you! As I saw myself speaking to thousands and thousands of people around the world I was overwhelmed. My question to my Creator was simply, "God, how am I going to do all of this?" One question seemed to lead to another, "Who is going to help me?" "How am I going to publish a book?" "How am I going to learn how to run a business?" The vision was so huge I knew I couldn't do it by myself! My evaluation of where I was at that very moment made it seem almost impossible. I was a prosecuting attorney with no business or writing background. I didn't know any authors. Nor did I have the slightest clue where to begin. All I had was the huge vision!

The vision was so overpowering, I forgot I had one other thing. I had a promise from my Creator that He was going to send people to take care of me. In other words, He was going to provide everything I needed to make this vision a successful reality. Because I am faith-based, I believed in the promise and started my journey by searching for some basic knowledge. My search wasn't as exciting as the vision had been. I had no clue where to start to make my vision a reality. What I did know was I could find a book on almost everything I needed to get started at my local bookstore. When I visited the bookstore there were plenty of books on how to write books, how to find an agent, how to write proposals and the difference between self-publishing versus traditional publishing deals. I sat on the floor flipping through every single one of them trying to determine which ones I should buy. The more I read the more I became overwhelmed. Writing a book and getting it published was going to come with a tremendous price. It was going to take time and money. I didn't have a lot of either one.

After divorcing my husband I started teaching extra speech classes to supplement my income. I was working full-time as a prosecutor in addition to my community involvement. Time and money were both scarce. I decided I would set a writing schedule to help me manage my time wisely. I would write from seven to eleven on Saturday and Sunday mornings. I wouldn't take any phone calls. Only one break was permitted during the four-hour writing period. I had all of the chapter titles before I started writing the book. I wasn't sure how it was going to come together but I sat down at the computer said a prayer, and then started typing.

About a month into writing, *Everything Has A Price!* I took a Saturday off to support the Zora Neal Hurston Festival held in the historic town of Eatonville, Florida. This is a major event in Central Florida. Each year, the town of Eatonville celebrates the life and legacy of Zora who was a prolific African-American writer. The festival combines culture, art, literature, and music with great food for a weekend that is always educational in addition to a whole lot of fun. As I was strolling through the festival I saw a sorority sister of mine who owns Montsho bookstore. She had a booth with authors signing their books. I wanted to talk with them about their experiences as authors, but people kept coming up asking for their autographs.

I stood around the booth for a few minutes watching the authors greet their readers and autographing as they talked. My eyes lit up as one of the male authors got up to take a break. I immediately walked over to him to introduce myself. He told me his name was Ricc Rollins. Ricc would be a tremendous blessing down the road. He had written several novels. More importantly he had self-published them all. I shared with him I had started writing a book with no clue how it would become published. Ricc handed me his card while telling me he would be happy to talk with me about publishing options. I met two other authors at the festival who assured me I could make my vision a reality. None of them really gave me the answer to my major question: How do I do it?

When I returned home, I placed the writers' information in a folder labeled "contacts." The cards sat untouched for almost seven months while I continued to write the chapters in the book. During the writing process I visited publishing websites, wrote proposals, sent inquiries to agents and attended workshops. The more I learned, the more I questioned how the vision would become a reality. Let me give you an example.

I received numerous rejection letters from agents. They were always professional and supportive of my work. They would start off thanking me for my submission, then politely give me the bad news: they were not accepting my work for representation. The letters would always close with best wishes for success. Based on the rejection letters and my research if I was serious about this book getting published I was going to have to do it myself. I kept the rejection letters for motivation. The letters were a reminder that not everyone will believe in your possibilities or be able to help you make your vision a reality.

To self-publish a book you need to start a publishing company. I had no knowledge of how to run a company nor did I have a desire to become an entrepreneur. I was completely satisfied with my government job. Working for the government I didn't have to worry about accounting issues or supply issues. I was writing the book to be obedient to the vision, not to start a new career at twenty-eight-years old. There are many best selling authors who self-published their books before a major publisher picked them up. However, I was new to the literary arena and didn't know how common it was to start by self-publishing.

As I was nearing completion of the book, I became a little concerned about the logistics of publishing. When you get to a place on your journey where you think you can't do anymore or go any further, someone will always appear who can assist you with the next phase of your vision. Sometimes it will be someone who appeared to cross your path for just a brief moment. In my case, it was Ricc. One day I was pondering what to do next with this vision. Suddenly Ricc popped into my head! A little voice said, "Call the guy you met at the Zora Festival." I dug out the card excited about the possibility of speaking to him. Then another little voice reminded me I had been to a publishing workshop at Barnes and Noble which provided lots of good information but when I tried to follow up with the presenter, the number had been disconnected. I decided nothing beats a failure but a try.

As I dialed the number I realized I had no clue what I was really looking for. But where there is a vision, there is always provision. You don't need to figure out each step, just keep moving and watch the direction become clear. I started the conversation by telling Ricc where he had met me. He in a very deep business like manner asked me how could he help me. Good question!

If you think you are going to have all the answers when you take your leap of faith, let me save you some major disappointment. You will not know how to do half of what you need to know. When I started writing the book, I didn't know how to write a book by the literary world's standards. I had not taken any formal writing classes for publishing. In fact, I hated writing after law school. I did not have a literary agent, nor did I have a single company interested in publishing my book. The reality of the situation was grim. In spite of all that I didn't know, I am now a published author! I am meeting and signing with best selling authors in venues I never dreamed of. I didn't know how the vision was going to become a reality, and the catch is I didn't have to know how. I just needed to trust the process one day at a time. I am a perfect example of where there is a vision; there will always be provision!

When I saw the vision of me speaking to thousands of people, I couldn't begin to figure how I was goingto transition from a sex crimes prosecutor and adjunct professor of public speaking to a motivational speaker. Where would the people come from? How would I book speaking engagements? How would I market myself? How would I pay my bills if I left the State Attorney's Office? In looking back, I realize where I am today is a complete miracle. My life as a speaker and author is more than I ever imagined. I have been in national magazines, spoken to thousands of people and traveled the country. I am blessed beyond belief! Why? It's simple; I am doing something I had absolutely no clue how to do! All I had was a vision and the courage to trust the process.

The wonderful thing about having a vision is if you believe with all that is within you, and trust the process, everything you need will come to you in the proper timing. I can share this with you because I have seen it work time after time on my journey!

One of my favorite stories to share with audiences as I travel the country is the story about my visit to the White House. My mother worked in the recruiting office for the Orlando Police Department. She called me one day to ask about some employment opportunities for a young lady from Washington, DC. The young lady was looking for employment in the Central Florida law enforcement community. The young lady had a tremendous background. She was a Secret Service agent assigned to the White House. I told my mother about several agencies, which might be a nice transition for the agent. As we were ending the phone call my mother said it would be nice if I called her to answer any questions she might have in addition to talking to her about the various agencies.

When I called to speak with the agent, I didn't have anything in mind other than being a resource for her in the Central Florida Community. I asked her a few questions about her background so I could get a better feel of what agencies would be of interest to her. As she talked about her years of service with government I was very proud of her. She had traveled all over the world, tackled people who were trespassing on the White House lawn, and now she was an agent in the White House with President Bill Clinton. I have seen the secret service agents in action while attending functions where the President of the United States was speaking. But I have never had a full-blown conversation with an agent. This was kind of cool! I didn't ask any security questions, or make any jokes. I was intrigued by her work and was glad to be a resource!

We have all heard the phrase, "It is better to give than receive." There are times when I believe your journey will take you to places to test your ability to give in order for you to receive. The agent asked me about my work as a former prosecutor and about my speaking career. She closed the conversation by offering me a tour of the White House if I ever came to Washington, DC. Wow, I would love that!

I could see me walking the halls of the White House. I could feel me taking in the awesomeness of the history the structure holds. There was one challenge: When would I be in DC? The agent was looking for a job in Central Florida so what were the odds that I would be speaking in DC before she relocated? The answer lies in the title of this chapter. Where there is a vision, there is always provision! I had visualized me standing in the White House. The vision would become a reality, but the path that led me to the White House was totally unexpected!

Months after my conversation with the agent, I arranged to share a booth with the Central Florida Association of Black Journalists at the National Conference in Phoenix, Arizona. The National Association of Black Journalists has some awesome workshops about various forms of media work. The program always includes a few sessions on writing and publishing. I was excited about attending the workshops, but I was also excited about the opportunity to promote my book with journalists from around the country.

Numerous journalists purchased my book during the three days I attended the convention. One young lady who had picked up my brochure returned to the booth after reading I was a motivational speaker. She came back to tell me she was looking for a speaker for the Federal Social Security Administration in Washington, D.C. The conference was in less than a month and her budget was minimal. They had a last minute slot to fill, could I do it? YES!!!

When I started my speaking career I accepted every offer I could because I needed the exposure. Every motivational speaker or successful business person will tell you when you find something you are so passionate about, you would do it for free, you have found your career. You have also found the thing that will make you wealthy. If you sit back, embrace the journey and enjoy the ride, it will provide incredible experiences. To be perfectly honest, when you embrace the journey instead of trying to figure it all out you will be able to see miracles happening daily.

I accepted the invitation to speak for the Federal Social Security Administration with no fee for my services. They only had a budget to pay for my flight, per diem and my accommodations for the event. This wasn't a bad deal. However, I was speaking for free which meant I was praying I would sell some books at the event to profit from the trip.

Remember, nothing just happens! The invitation to the Social Security Administration came one week before I received an email inviting authors from around the country to participate in a pavilion at the Black Congressional Caucus Convention in DC. The Convention was to be held on the same weekend as my event for the Social Security Administration. I found out I would be a moderator instead of a workshop speaker for the Social Security Administration. This changed the picture a little because the amount of exposure as a moderator for a panel is very different than what I would receive as a speaker. The book sales would also be very different.

The authors pavilion at the Congressional Caucus was not a conflicting event so my prayer was it would provide a forum to generate both exposure and revenue. I asked the Social Security Administration to make arrangements for my flight to return to Orlando on Sunday instead of Friday. They agreed.

Once the plans were confirmed, I remembered the secret service agent's offer for a tour of the White House. I called to inform her I would be in DC for a few days. She was delighted! The agent offered to pick me up from the airport. What seemed like a noble gesture would end up being a lifesaver!

The week before the trip I started stressing because I had no money. This was not the first time I had cut it close while traveling. Normally, I set a hundred dollar minimum to have on a trip. I travel with very little cash, but if I have at least one hundred dollars in the bank, I can usually cover an emergency if need be. On the Monday before the trip I only had fifty-four dollars. I was scheduled to leave on Thursday. I couldn't cancel the trip. I was struggling with a range of fears. If the agent couldn't pick me up from the airport, a ride in the taxi from the airport to my hotel would be almost thirty dollars. That would leave me with twenty-four dollars to eat and get back to the airport. I felt the panic setting in. Every vision has a voice behind it. I heard a calm voice saying,

Lucy: Veraunda, just go, you will be ok. This is a wonderful opportunity!

Keisha: Girl, don't you dare go romping to DC without money. What if something happens? This is an opportunity all right, an opportunity to wind up stranded in a strange city!

Lucy: You believe in a God who will never leave or forsake you. You must stand firmly in that belief.

Keisha: I can't argue with that premise, but what I can say is God gives you wisdom and it is not wise to jump on a plane with fifty-four dollars for three days.

Lucy: If you are living by faith, this isn't about fifty-four dollars it is about giving God an opportunity to work a miracle with the fifty-four dollars.

I called the secret service agent on Wednesday evening to confirm my arrival with her. She promised she would pick me up on the curb. We exchanged cell phone numbers, "just in case." As I stepped on the plane, I said a small prayer, "Lord, I don't know what this trip is all about, but I am going with the faith that you will not only take care of me while I am in DC, but you will reveal to me your purpose for this trip."

It is indeed a wonderful experience to see and hear your vision become a reality. On the plane ride I was in complete peace for a simple reason, no matter what happened in DC, there was no turning back for me. I was on the plane. I would have to literally "ride this journey out." The basics were provided, I knew for sure I had a plane ticket back home. I knew for sure I had a place to stay. Well, I was supposed to have a place to stay. This is where the first miracle happened. The secret service agent was a few minutes late picking me up. Part of me wanted to panic:

Keisha: Girl, I told you!

Lucy: Oh, no you don't! You will not start with your negativity. Veraunda just give the woman a chance to get here.

Keisha: I can't believe you are a former prosecutor letting a complete stranger pick you up with no background check! You have no secret code. This woman could be a serial killer for all you know. She might be wanted by the FBI and that is why she is serving secretly!

Lucy: Keisha if you don't stop this foolishness! You are literally crazy. How do you think of this stuff?

Your mind can take you to places you know are totally ridiculous. It is the fear driving your mind to question every little circumstance as if the world was coming to an end today. Keisha wasn't crazy because **I know I am not crazy!** We all have these wild thoughts, which make very little sense. Most of us are afraid to articulate them. I, on the other hand, have learned to listen to these voices carefully. The vision's voice is always one of calm and reason. When I hear panic or negativity speaking, I know it is my fear challenging my faith. The ultimate decision is in my control. The voices debate the issue for me to decide my fate. There will always be a voice telling you to settle. But there will always be a voice telling you to create the life you want. Your challenge is choosing to believe one of the voices. There is no middle ground when your dreams are on the line. Either you are going to listen to the voice of your vision or you are going to listen to the voice of doubt telling you why you can't do it, why you shouldn't do it and why it won't work. I chose to listen to the voice of my vision. As Keisha was trying to get a word in, I saw an African American woman standing next to a brand new White Mercedes Benz.

Lucy: Oooh, not only is the agent picking you up, she is picking you up in a beautiful Mercedes Benz. This is just the beginning of the trip. We are off to a very good start! Just enjoy the ride!

Keisha: It is a nice car, but...

Lucy: Why does there always have to be a but with you? You drive me crazy!

Keisha: All I'm trying to say is once we get back home we will be able to relax.

Lucy: I totally disagree; we need to take in all of the experiences on the journey. Your destiny is being created one moment at a time. Veraunda, if you don't embrace it, you will wake up one day and realize you missed all of the miracles that were happening on a daily basis. Get in the car and let the good times roll. We are going to take it one day at a time knowing your vision will always come with provision.

It was a gorgeous day in DC. The agent gave me a scenic tour of the city pointing out various landmarks on the way to the hotel. When we drove past the White House I said a prayer of thanks. "Lord, I know there are great things in store for me. Thank you for getting me here safely. Thank you for the ride from the airport with the agent. Thank you for putting me in a position to travel the country making a difference." I am a firm believer in giving thanks for each miracle no matter how big or small. I have found it keeps me focused on the positive situations instead of the fear that constantly tries to sneak up in your spirit.

As we pulled up to the historic hotel in downtown DC, the agent pointed out I would be staying across the street from the Treasury Department. There were numerous other governmental agencies within walking distance. The agent helped me with my bags. I expressed my gratitude, and offered to pay her gas money (my mother always taught me to be prepared to pay for gas when people gave me a ride). The agent refused the money, then told me she would wait for me to get checked in before she left. I assured her I would be fine indicating I would call her first thing in the morning to check in with her about the tour of the White House. The agent insisted upon waiting until I was checked in before leaving me alone in downtown DC. This is where the next phase of the miracle took place.

I entered the plush hotel looking forward to taking a shower followed by a nice little nap. The bellman quickly took my bags while greeting me with a warm smile. When I approached the counter, the clerk asked for my name. The room was indeed ready; all he needed was a credit card to secure the room. Excuse me? Prior to leaving I had confirmed with the SSA they would have the room taken care of. I had also been honest telling them I didn't have extra funds to pay for the room first. They assured me it was not a problem. I had been traveling for almost a year speaking. On most occasions, the group bringing me in took care of the accommodations. Very rarely had I needed a credit card to secure the room. My credit card was only used for incidentals like food and phone calls. The rooms at this hotel were over two hundred dollars a night. For three nights they would need almost eight hundred dollars approval on my credit card. As NASA would say, "DC...we have a problem!"

I tried explaining to the clerk the room should be listed under a block with the Federal Social Security Administration. He said it was, however, he still needed a credit card to guarantee the room. I questioned why this was the case if there were notes showing the administration would pay for the room. He said it was just the hotel's policy.

Keisha: Now do you believe me? You have fifty-four dollars to your name. What are you going to do?

Lucy: Don't panic, you haven't been brought to DC to be stranded. Let's call the client.

This was an excellent idea, except when I tried the office, I received the voicemail. The voice mail said the office was closed due to the staff attending the seminar. I tried the cell phone of the person who made my arrangements. I was greeted by voice mail again. I tried to sound calm while I left her a message asking her to call me as soon as possible.

I tried to negotiate my way to a reasonable solution. If the clerk would allow me to check in, I was positive the event coordinator would be available this evening. She could clear all of this up. I could leave my drivers license with him at the desk. However, I didn't have a way to provide an eight hundred dollar guarantee. The clerk apologized, but said he could not change the policy. I asked for the manager. Nonchalantly he replied, "I am the manager."

Keisha: This is exactly why I didn't want you to take this trip! Now you are stuck!!! To make matters worse, you don't know a soul here nor can you reach the client to get her to assist you. You are stranded with no money!

Lucy: Keisha is wrong. You are not stranded. The agent is outside waiting to make sure you got checked in. Go explain to tell her what is going on.

Keisha: *What is she going to do, give you her credit card to guarantee the room? You don't know her and she doesn't know you! She has already done her good deed for today. She got you to the hotel. Her volunteer work is done!*
Lucy: *Veraunda, go back to the car.*

Keisha: *No, I think you should just sit in the lobby until the client calls you back or comes to get you.*

Before I knew it I was walking down the large Oriental rug centering the hard wood floors. The bellman followed closely behind me with my luggage. The mirrors on both sides of the hall made me seem really small under the gorgeous chandeliers. When I reached the doors I felt the embarrassment of the situation hit me. The agent asked me what was wrong. I explained the guarantee policy. She agreed with me, it was an unusual practice when there was a governmental agency that had made the arrangements. She had traveled around the world with presidents for the past eleven years. When it was a government account, the guarantee had always been for incidentals only.

Without blinking an eye, she grabbed my bags while telling me I was going home with her. She needed to pick up her daughter from the sitter, then I could join her family for dinner. I felt awful! I was becoming a burden to someone who was trying to do a kind deed by picking me up at the airport. She lived in the suburbs of DC, near Baltimore. Lord, what was I going to do now? The agent told me to relax, she didn't mind at all. It would all work itself out. Keisha was trying to say something, but I couldn't deal with her at the moment. I was focusing on being thankful that the agent hadn't left me at the hotel. I was thankful she had a warm spirit. I was thankful she was taking care of me in this apparent disaster.

As we drove to the outskirts of DC, she pointed out various buildings of importance giving me a mini-history of the city. She also talked about her job with the Secret Service. She told me how she started with the agency, the various places she had been and how much I enjoyed her job. Working for the Secret Service sounded intriguing and challenging.

When we pulled into the driveway of her home I said, "Wow, this is really nice!" It was a large two-story home. The agent gave me a tour of the house. There were five bedrooms, two-car garage, a basement that seemed like a mini-home, a small workout room complete with a treadmill and television. We ended the tour by walking out to the deck which overlooked a beautiful pool in the backyard. Well, if I was stuck this was not a bad place to be stranded! I was very comfortable with the agent. Her kids instantly livened up the house. Her daughter came down stairs with a doll for me to play with. Her son was busy trying to tell her what happened in school. Life was taking care of each of us.

Time passed quickly. Before I knew it was after five in the evening. Where was my contact at the SSA? Why hadn't she called me yet? The panic creeped back in. I apologized to the agent as she made arrangements for us to eat Chinese food for dinner. Chinese sounded great! I was definitely hungry! She assured me she was enjoying my company. I was concerned about altering her whole day because of the problem with the hotel. She moved right along saying, "girl, you are my guest, relax. If she doesn't call you back, you can stay here tonight. We have plenty of room. I'll get you where you need to be in the morning. It's not a problem." She quickly changed the subject back to her Central Florida job search.

About twenty minutes later my cell phone rang. It was my host from the SSA. She apologized for the tardiness in returning my call. The conference had kept her extremely busy. She had not had an opportunity to check her voice mail. I explained the hotel situation to her. She asked me where I was. I told her about the agent who had graciously agreed to be my host since my arrival. The SSA employee told me she was working on her master's degree at a nearby university. She wasn't going to be finished until after nine tonight. She asked me if it would be a problem for me to stay with the agent until she was finished with class then she would come to pick me up. The agent said it was absolutely fine with her. I felt a little peace having talked to the SSA host. But I would be glad to get into my room, shower and go to sleep.

After dinner we watched television. The time seem to fly by. The SSA host came to pick me up. She apologized for the mess at the hotel. She assured me during our drive back to downtown Washington

DC, she would clear it all up. That was positive thinking! When we arrived at the hotel, the manager I spoke with earlier was still there. After much discussion we ended up in the same situation. The manager refused to release the room without a credit card. The SSA host said they had problems in the past. This was the last straw! It was almost eleven now. I was exhausted and so was the SSA host. She was getting frustrated. We decided the solution was to just leave this hotel. She had a suite at the Hilton and if I didn't mind sharing a room with her she would deal with this hotel after the conference was over. I was so tired, that as long as there was a bed, I would be happy. We left the historic hotel for the Hilton down the street. It was a very nice hotel about five minutes away. The suite had a living room with a television in addition to a sofa bed. My host slept in the living room. I was more than ready for a good night's rest in the king-size bed in the bedroom. We had an early morning not to mention long day ahead of us.

I attended some workshops Friday morning, then enjoyed the luncheon with SSA employees from around the country. My panel was immediately after lunch. It was packed! As the moderator, the time flew quickly. I was praying I would sell some books. I was disappointed when I sold less than five books after the event. This trip was not working out the way I had intended.

Keisha: You should have listened to me! When are you going to learn? I have your best interest at heart. I am not trying to ruin your dream! I'm trying to create some stability in our lives. Maybe this is not the right timing for you to pursue the speaking. Perhaps you should go back to work for a couple of years, build an audience, then try it again.

Lucy: NO! You should just keep taking one step at a time. Think about this, you are in DC as a moderator for the Federal Social Security Office! This is a huge invitation. It will open doors for you. Keep in mind you will also be signing at the Congressional Black Caucus tomorrow. It will all work itself out. The vision never leaves you without provision!

Keisha: Lucy, there are days when I believe you are the crazy one! She sold five books which is eighty dollars. She is sharing a room with the SSA host where is the silver lining that you see?

Lucy: In the cloud that you are seeing! The hotel is very nice. Tonight she'll have the room to herself. At least she sold some books. She has eighty dollars more than she started with. It's about finding the good in every situation. She is not out on the street; she has been taken care of every minute of this trip. If it wasn't for you and your constant negative outlook on the world we would be much better!

Keisha: This is not negativity it is reality!

Lucy: Have you ever thought that things are not always what they appear to be!

Lucy is right. Many times things will appear to be one way, when they are totally different. That afternoon when I returned to the hotel I called the Secret Service agent. She told me she would call me a little later on to set up the tour of the White House. Around seven I decided it was getting late, so I started getting ready for bed. It had been a long two days. I was not only disappointed in the low book sales, but it didn't look like I was going to get that tour after all.

Keisha: It is after seven p.m. on Friday, the White House is closed! I told you not to get your hopes up. Now you are disappointed. You need to stop getting yourself so worked up with all these possibilities!

Lucy: You don't leave until Sunday, anything is possible between now and then! Just be patient, don't try to predict everything that is going to happen on the journey. Just enjoy it. Whatever the outcome, you can't go wrong. You are taken care of.

Keisha: But what about the vision to see the White House to feel the history and all that jazz. See even you have abandoned our vision!

Lucy: Nope, you are wrong Keisha! I haven't abandoned the vision, I'm confident Veraunda will get there. The agent appears to be a woman of her word. What I am abandoning is the worry and the fear that you constantly create in Veraunda's head!

While Keisha and Lucy were debating the issue, I drifted off to sleep. I felt myself jump when my cell phone started ringing. It was the agent calling to tell me she was on her way to pick me up. I opened my eyes trying to focus on the clock next to the bed. What time was it? It was a little after eight on Friday night. Was she kidding me? What were we going to do at the White House this time of night? Everybody knows the White House closes at night. I was sure security was going to be super tight. Isn't it amazing how once you have listened to negativity for a period of time, you don't need the voice anymore. You become the voice. The voice of the vision has to constantly struggle with you. In my case, it's not that I don't believe in the vision. Quite the contrary, I struggle with the emotions that come with trying to live your dream when it doesn't look like you thought it would look.

I once heard a pastor say, when God shows you a vision, He never reveals how the vision will become a reality. He wants to see how much faith you have during the process. The process is where the work comes in. The process is paying the price for what you believe in. The process is what will make you question your ability and your sanity. But the process is also where you will experience incredible growth. I can tell you from my own journey, if the process had been shown to me, I would not have stepped out of my comfortable job as a prosecutor to struggle with finances, friends, family and my own inner emotions. It is the blind faith that will propel you to places you never imagined!

As I started getting dressed, I felt my heart beating a little quicker than normal. Although, I didn't know what my tour would consist of, I was getting excited. I was going to the White House! I dressed up in a nice brown skirt and matching blouse. I took the rollers out of my hair then pulled my shoulder length hair back from my face. I decided to accent the outfit with a nice multi-colored animal print scarf. I put on a light coat of lipstick. There was no telling who I might meet tonight. If President Bill and First Lady Hillary were home, I wanted to make a good impression. As this thought crossed my mind, I giggled to myself. (Maybe I was crazy!) As I slipped into my brown heels, the cell phone rang notifying me the agent was downstairs. I slipped my camera into my purse, took one last look in the full-length mirror on the bathroom door and hurried out the room.

The agent was downstairs in the white Mercedes. The bellman opened the car door for me. I smiled as I imagined the possibilities! What if one day I was constantly chauffeured from event to event? What if, one day I was invited to the White House to speak? What if I was able to afford whatever I wanted? One day, this whole experience would be a faint memory of how things "used to be!" My mind was racing all over the place with "what ifs?" The screen in my mind replayed my original vision. I saw the crowd of thousands listening to me speak. I couldn't hear what I was saying but I was moving about on the huge platform. In the vision, it wasn't just the crowd loving every minute of it! I was loving every minute of it with them! My spirit was clear, one day I would be an international speaker traveling the world!

The agent brought me back to the present by showing me where the ambassadors from other countries reside when they visit. Wow, I never thought about where ambassadors stay. I guessed they stayed in hotels like everyone else. Wrong! They stay across the street from the White House. Security is amazing in the White House complex. As we entered the property I was like a little girl in the Magic Kingdom of Disney for the first time! I took everything in! The security gates looked much bigger up close. There were cameras everywhere! My host agent started to introduce me to her employees. They were all very cheerful and pleasant. It was almost nine at night. They were certainly alert. They asked me to enter the electronic metal detector. My purse was put through another machine. Oooh, was I going to get in trouble for having a camera?

My host agent was the sergeant, so I was able to keep the camera. This was vital. I really wanted to be able to capture my visit to the White House. After all, what if President Bill and First Lady Hillary were home? I couldn't miss that photo opportunity now could I? After I cleared security, I was given a visitor's badge. We exited the security office which lead me to the grounds of the White House of the United States of America! Wow, it was much larger than I expected! My host agent told me she was going to give me a full tour of everything but the private quarters. That part of the White House is off limits. We entered the West Wing of the White House. It was absolutely breath taking! Everything is rich with history! The furniture is rich with tradition. The paintings and pictures on the wall tell amazing stories. The security was also telling. There was a k-9 unit on the grounds at this late hour.

There were numerous agents stationed at various posts around the house. They too seemed to have their own stories. I had all the time in the world tonight. The curiosity in me wanted to hear how they found careers as Secret Service Agents. Most indicated it had been their dream. Each night when they reported, they were walking on the grounds of the White House! What a job! Just like every job there was a price. They were expected to pay the ultimate price of their lives, to protect the President and the first family. Some told stories of dangerous encounters. Others had seen very little action on the grounds. Wow, this was indeed an awesome experience. As I talked to each agent, I was reminded how each of us at our core is just a servant during our time here. I was reminded no matter how small or big your vision, it can become a reality. There are thousands of people whose careers are a reflection of their dreams.

As we traveled the grounds my spirit was humbled. My vision had brought me here. Simply, being who I was had brought me here. I could not help thinking this was just the beginning of the journey. I was thinking of all the possibilities. I started listing the places I wanted to go. One day, I would be having dinner with Presidents and traveling the world living my dream. Tonight's visit to the White House was just the opening act to confirm, yes, it is possible!

We walked the grounds on what had to be one of the nicest nights in our nation's capital. There was a clear sky with a light chill in the air. The lights from the monuments seemed to sparkle as the busy district set a perfect backdrop for my tour. We visited the Rose Garden, onsite florist shop, the East Wing, the kitchen, the bowling alley, and the Oval Office. Visitors aren't allowed in the Oval Office. However, you may look in the office from the doorway, which was roped off. The agent assigned at this post, gave me the history of the office. It was intriguing. I learned when the president leaves office, the items that are given to him during his tenure as president is the property of the U.S. Government. So many of the paintings, statues, even the hand carved desk had been gifts from countries, or individuals over the past hundred years.

We ended the tour in the pressroom. I think this is when it really hit me! I was standing in the White House at thirty years old because I had taken a leap of faith to live my dreams by writing the book and speaking. The pressroom is much smaller than it appears on television. There is a lot of computer and audio-visual equipment in the back of the room which is about a thirty-seat, theater style room. There are lights facing the small staging area which has the White House Seal centered on the podium. I asked my host if I could just stand behind the podium. She said sure. I asked her if she would take a picture to capture this moment. (In reality it would serve as proof on the days it was a faint memory that I was really here!) As I posed for the picture behind the podium, I couldn't help thinking how appropriate that I was standing behind a podium. This was a place I was very comfortable. It was where I had been since I was twelve years old. I said a small prayer of thanks for my Creator using this visit to Washington, DC to whisper to my spirit. *"Veraunda, there is no limit to what you can experience while on this earth! Whatever you can envision, can become a reality! Just believe! Don't ever give up! Hold onto this moment, reflect on what I originally showed you! You will be speaking to millions around the world...and I will ALWAYS give you provision to match the vision!"*

My host must have wondered what was going on in my mind. Tears had formed in my eyes. I told her this entire trip was a faith experience. It started with me worrying before I left about money. It continued with whether she would arrive at the airport to pick me up, then the hotel situation, not to mention the disappointing book sales at the conference. Then to top it all off is when I didn't think I was going to get the tour of the Whitehouse because it was getting late. Each time my faith was tested, the voices would start chatting, but I was OK. I was better than OK. I was standing in the White House. Wow! Things have a way of just working themselves out. My host smiled. She seemed to know exactly how I felt. She had traveled the world with the Secret Service. She too, was a product of a vision. She told me the travel had been fun, tiring, and sometimes challenging. My remarks had reminded her that despite the situation, she had always been OK. It was quite an amazing moment to realize despite our own fears and weaknesses we were both standing in the

White House of the United States of America just because we had a vision.

On your journey you will experience lack of focus, frustration and fear. At those times, you must take a moment to stand still and reflect on the vision. Let the voice of the vision speak to you. It will remind you no matter how bad the situation looks at that moment, your vision will provide everything you need, when you need it. There have been many times as a business owner I have freaked out with worry or fear. Then the calm voice of my vision will remind me of simple provisions, like I am still here. I have NEVER been in a situation that hasn't worked out. There has always been provision working right along with my vision. The vision becomes a reality because you don't give up. The vision becomes a reality because you expect the provision to always show up just in time! I want to leave you with this, "Thought that makes a difference!"

Angels Appear When You Least Expect Them!

How many times have you been in a situation that seemed hopeless? Have you ever just stopped and said this can't be happening to me? Well, I am living proof that angels will appear when you need them most!

I traveled to Memphis for a conference. Simply put, it was a disaster. I spent my own money to attend and nothing was as it had been promised. When I was dropped off at the airport I was glad to be coming back home! My flight was scheduled to leave around 7p.m. The last thing I expected was the ticket agent to tell me my flight was canceled and there were no other flights to Orlando. The only thing I could do was try to check with the other airlines.

I immediately panicked. This could not be happening! I had a paid speaking event in Orlando for Sprint on Saturday morning at 10:00am. The first flight to Orlando wasn't until 9:00 in the morning. There was no way I could make it, no way for me to call the contact person in Orlando, and no way I could afford a same day ticket even if someone had a flight. I ran from counter to counter with my bags in tow. After standing in line for 30 minutes, I learned that most flights left Memphis before 6p.m. I had tears in my eyes. I know God did not bring me this far to leave me! I said a quick prayer and told the ticket agent I had to get home! He checked the computer, and lo and behold there was one flight...leaving at 6:30 on US Airways. But he said I'd better hurry; it was already boarding. The time was 6:15!!!

I ran to the US Airways counter. The ticket agent asked for my voucher from the flight that was canceled. I didn't have one! She told me she wasn't going to hold the flight. I ran back over to the other airline, went straight to the counter and proceeded to give the woman hell. (Yep, I am being honest.) Of course she gave me attitude right back. I had to get on that plane! Another ticket agent intervened taking me over to security. She was going to run me to the gate with the travel voucher in hand with the hopes I would be able to get on the plane. I was saying prayers for both forgiveness and for mercy!

When we reached security she realized she had left her security ID back in her office. What else could go wrong? What about, take off your shoes, take the laptop out of the bag, go back through the metal detector. Every minute that passed my heart raced faster. Would you believe I was the only person in security at the airport? There was no line, just me! Couldn't they tell I was in a hurry? Didn't they know I was panicking? Oh my gosh!!! By the time the ticket agent returned I was really in tears. Out of nowhere, a tall, handsome African American pilot appeared. He asked me where I was going. I couldn't talk because I knew I was close to losing it. The ticket agent told him I was headed for Orlando. With a calm voice he said, "I'm the pilot of that flight. The plane can't leave without me and I won't leave without her."

He told me to leave my bags with him and he would bring them to the gate. I should just run to get checked in. It was odd, when I arrived at the gate I was scanned again and my backpack was searched. Once again I was the only person in the entire gate area. This was incredible! The ticket agent at the gate said he would have to see if he could get me on the flight. Since he wasn't moved by my sense of emergency, he politely finished closing out his confirmed passengers in the computer first. Just about this time, the pilot walked up, telling me very simply, "I said, I wasn't going to leave without you." I had to hold onto his words; they were my only hope. It seemed like an eternity but I was finally permitted to board the plane. I ran down the breezeway. Guess who was sitting in the cockpit looking back? Yep, the pilot. He smiled and said, "OK, now we can depart." I started crying again while saying thank you to him. I hurried into a seat while the flight attendant told me, "We were waiting for you." I looked at my watch realizing the pilot should have been on the plane long before I saw him in the security area. This plane should have left ten minutes ago! Wow, my angel had appeared when I needed him the most! He really did have wings and could fly!

When we landed in Charlotte for my connecting flight, I asked to see him. I had written a thank you note in addition to autographing a book for him during the flight. He came out in the breezeway to greet me. I told him he had no idea what he had just done for me. As I gave him the book, he looked at the picture then said "Wow! This is you!" I told him tonight, he had been my angel. He gave me a huge hug while saying, "God bless you!" My response? "He already has!"

When all hope seems to be gone, just say a prayer and watch your angel appear! God really does comes through when you need him the most He uses people like you and me everyday to make a difference in the lives of others! Thank you Michael Law of US Airways for being my angel!" God uses people like you and me everyday to be the provision for someone else's vision!

Apply the lesson in this chapter to your life:

What do you <u>think</u> you need to make your vision a reality?

Do you have everything you need? YES or NO

Do you believe enough in your vision and your Creator that you will trust the process? YES or NO

List at least three situations or times when you didn't know how you were going to make it, yet provision was made for you:

You Don't Have To Settle!

Know when to walk away!

Have you ever been on a path you just knew was right? It was the path that would lead you to the promise land? This path appears to be lined with gold bricks. If you just follow the yellow brick road you know you will be rich and famous, or at least wealthy and happy. It usually starts out with a simple idea. You get extremely excited about the idea and more ideas pop into your head. Ahhhh this is THE ONE! You wonder why you hadn't thought about this earlier! You are energized! You can't sleep at night thinking about the possibilities. You start planning the journey in your head. You begin the process of walking down the path that will free you from financial debt, office politics and allow you to live your dreams!

Well, I stumbled on that path right after writing my first book. The Women's National Basketball Association (WNBA) granted Orlando a franchise in 1999. The team was named the Orlando Miracle. One of my good friends suggested we go to a couple of games to support female athletics. I'll be honest; I like sports but I am just a spectator who enjoys the social aspects of games. I can't tell you much about the rules of the game, but I am familiar with the gist of basketball.

The one thing I enjoyed about dancing and twirling flags on the drill team in high school, was the excitement of the games and cheering the home team to victory. So I thought this would be a good social outing for me. The tickets were very affordable and the season only lasted three months during the summer. I went to the first game and was hooked. I cheered, hollered, screamed and even networked. I wanted to go back for the next game. One game turned into an entire season.

One particular game, a conversation about women's athletics turned into a huge light bulb of an idea. I was sitting with a friend who was also an attorney. The conversation started with us talking about the player's salaries, and ended with us wondering about their representation. Specifically, we wondered how many female agents represented female athletes.

The question drove us crazy! We were excited and hungry for more information. I was still working for the government as a prosecutor. My colleague had her own law firm and was doing quite well for herself. She was intelligent and had a diverse background as a lawyer. I had the utmost respect for her as a professional. We started doing our homework. We called the local WNBA franchise. We spoke with the assistant coach. She gave us exactly what we needed to start on the path. She told us there were very few female agents in women's sports. This could be a niche. She also gave us some great leads and contacts. There were a few words of caution given as well. This was a male-dominated field. It had been hard for women to break into the sports business. Women athletes did not make half the salaries their male counterparts were making. In otherwords, we would not become wealthy by representing female athletes alone. We needed to figure out how we were going to be different.

The thought of a challenge was exciting! Our brains began processing the information quickly. We were on to something and it was something big! We were going to be different just because of who we were. We were two African American attorneys who had ten years of combined experience. I had been a criminal prosecutor for almost five years. But what I really brought to the table was my background in communications. I had been speaking professionally since the age of twelve. I had been a radio personality and a talk show host. I was an adjunct professor of public speaking. I had just started speaking on the national speaking circuit. I knew there was a lot of untapped income in the speaking industry. So if we could help market the players as speakers, this would be my kind of business!

I met my colleague when I started at the State Attorney's Office. There were only three other African American female Attorneys other than myself at the time. My colleague immediately made herself available. She was friendly and we connected quickly. We stayed in contact after she left the State Attorney's office for a job with a private law firm. We made lunch appointments so we could stay abreast of the others' plight. My colleague was gaining a wealth of knowledge about various areas of the laws. When we started talking about women's athletics she was a partner in her own law firm. I was proud of her accomplishments and in awe of her courage to start her own firm before turning thirty years old.

Youth has a way of making you feel invincible. The more we talked about women athletes needing women agents, the more we felt we were the answer. We were clear this would be a tremendous undertaking. Just organizing the company and figuring out the world of sports agents was going to be a challenge. But when we looked at our backgrounds we were sure we could do it. In fact, we were positive *we could do it better than anybody else.*

My colleague was thirty-one. I was twenty-nine-years-old. She had played sports, had negotiated contracts, been through mediation and started her own firm. This background would serve us well in several areas. She would be able to help us structure the company and negotiate contracts. She would also be able to use her background as an athlete to help us see the business through the player's eyes. She could focus on statistics, athletic talent and recruiting.

My background as a prosecutor gave me some negotiating skills, but my communications skills would be the real asset for the company. I would be instrumental in speech coaching and public relations for the players. We would hire an image consultant, so our clients would be marketable both on and off the court. We would be different. We would be a full service-firm for female athletes.

We started having regular business meetings. We talked almost daily. Every conversation was filled with smiles and excitement. We decided early on our company would represent women athletes exclusively. As we followed up on the leads we were provided, everyone seemed to think we were on to something big. The possibilities were endless!

As the organization meetings progressed, one thing was clear. This was going to be a lot of work! The hardest part would be recruiting players. Recruiting didn't appeal to me at all. There were several concerns I had. First, I was already starting to travel with my company, EHAP Inc. as a speaker and consultant. Second, the rules for sports agents were very strict. Just getting the athletes to speak with you would be a real challenge. Signing them would be a bigger challenge. Third, there are so many colleges, so many players that getting the top draft picks would be a challenge. Based on what I know now, most top female basketball players have hired male agents who have an established track record with the male athletes. Remember, professional women's sports in the year 1999 were still a relatively new arena.

As if the recruiting wasn't a big enough challenge, professionally each one of us had to meet certain guidelines. The State of Florida required us to take an agent's exam in addition to paying almost one thousand dollars in fees. We studied regularly. This was new material for us. I guess the state figured they were really giving us a break, because if you were a lawyer you only had to take a fifty-question exam, versus all other applicants taking a one-hundred-question exam. I thought I am a lawyer; I shouldn't have to take another exam for the rest of my life after the two and a half day bar exam! Regardless of my personal opinion, we both took the exam very seriously. We met weekly to go through the material and try to digest the various National Collegiate Athletic Association (NCAA) rules. It was a bit complicated, because there are different rules that apply to different divisions. We highlighted, underlined, and outlined the material.

In the midst of studying for the exam, we found out the Players Association for the Women's National Basketball Association (WNBPA) had a five hundred dollar fee and an application packet almost as thick as the State of Florida's application. Typing the applications was a chore all by itself. But to top it all off, the Players Association was having a mandatory meeting in New York City a few weeks before our exam. Now, at any other point a trip to the Big Apple would have been right up our alley. But the timing of this meeting was challenging for several reasons. I was still rebounding from a divorce and I was living from paycheck to paycheck. We both were trying to study for this exam and finally, we weren't officially sports agents. In Florida, you are not a sports agent until the Department of Business & Regulation grants you a license, which would not be until after we passed the exam. So we had to call for an ethical opinion from the Florida Bar before we could attend the meeting.

When I look back on the situation, I am amazed by how creative we were with so little financial resources. We found discounted airline tickets through a friend who worked for the airlines. We scrounged up the WNBPA fee somehow and met the deadline to register for the mandatory agents meeting. This meeting was vital to our careers as sports agents because if you are not registered and in good standing with the players association you can not represent any players in the league. So when they said mandatory, what they really meant was if you don't come, you can't be an agent in this league. With no choice in the matter, we were on our way to New York for the meeting.

One of the first rules of business is know your partner. As a lawyer, I had heard many horror stories about partnerships. Some of the worst stories were of friends who started law firms together. My business partner and I had discussed this phenomenon several times. We both had concerns, but we reassured each other, we would be different. We both had impeccable work ethic. We both were intelligent. We would compliment each other. Where one was weak, the other appeared to be strong. We would communicate openly and honestly. We would do everything as a team. Our partnership would work.

We had our first disagreement trying to take our first trip together. Sometimes the excitement can blind you. You are so enthusiastic about your possibilities you forget to implement wisdom about basic realities. In our case, I knew my business partner could be a little tardy at times. In most cases I arrived before she did. For business meetings this had never been a problem. I was just happy to be there. I am a workaholic by all definitions, so I would always have something with me that I could work on. This meant I could occupy my time wisely while waiting.

On the night before the trip we did what women do. We talked about the trip, we compared wardrobe selections, we giggled, and we discussed the possibilities. We were excited! Watch out New York, here we come. I was designated as the airport chauffeur, which meant picking her up at her home, then leaving my vehicle at the airport. As a frequent traveler, I have no problem with driving to the airport. It really does make life a lot easier to have your car there when you return home. Our flight was leaving early in the morning. I am a very punctual person. It really irritates me when others are not ready or tardy for appointments. Almost everyone, who knows me, can tell you when I say six o'clock, I really mean five fifty five. (I get this trait from my father.)

When the alarm clock started spewing out songs to awaken me, I was already awake. I was just laying there. I was too excited to sleep and probably too afraid of oversleeping to really get a good night's rest. I called my partner immediately to make sure she was up. She said she was, but it didn't sound like it. I told her I would call her as I was leaving my house so she could govern herself accordingly. I did just that. But guess what happened when I arrived at her house. I had to wait! Now, in the big scheme of things, five or ten minutes aren't a big deal, but in airports five or ten minutes can cause you to miss your flight.

I was frustrated the whole drive to the airport. I was feeling rushed which I hate! When we arrived at the airport and had to circle for what seemed like an eternity to find parking, I was pissed. A word to the wise, don't ever ask what else can go wrong when you are running late for an airline trip. We practically ran to the terminal. The line for counter check in was long to say the least, but I had this funny feeling we may not be able to check the bags at the gate. My partner said, she thought we could check bags at the gate. My travel experience said stay at the counter. I didn't want to take the risk. By now I am pissed with her because she made us late, so I ignored her and chose to stand in the line for counter check in. She continued through the terminal while calling back she would meet me at the gate.

It was a good choice on my part to go to the counter. A ticket agent made a last call for late passengers going to New York. I quickly stepped to the front of the line with my luggage. She processed the bags then told me to run to the gate. I took her advice seriously and literally ran through the terminal. When I arrived at the gate, huffing and puffing, my partner was no where in site. The flight was in the final boarding stages. I assumed she was already on the plane. I assumed wrong. There was no baggage check in available at the gate. (I told her so!) They sent her back to the main terminal to check her luggage in. She was literally the last person to get on the plane. I wanted to scream, *"See this is why being on time is so important! I bet next time you will listen to me won't you!"* But instead, I saw the sweat that had formed on her face, and the embarrassment in her eyes. The lesson was quite clear. Punctuality is a must when traveling. I vowed silently I would drive my own car and meet her at the airport for future trips.

The first few minutes of the trip were very quiet, but as the time passed, we began talking about our strategy for New York and quickly let by gones be bygones. The excitement overcame the morning's event. We started pondering the possibilities. We wondered whom we would meet and what we would learn. We would be sitting in a room with other sports agents from around the country. We had business cards designed for the trip. We had matching laptops to type on. We had nice briefcases to accent our professionalism. New York, here we come!

When you start thinking about the possibilities, it is you against the world! Your mind reminds you the world is huge! But because you are so excited you think you can conquer the world. I recall my partner and I saying, "The world of women's sports better get ready! They haven't seen anything like us!" There was some truth to that statement. However, we learned quickly you don't just conquer an empire over night.

When we arrived in New Jersey it was cold. We quickly put our leather jackets on. We had arranged for an associate to pick us up at the Newark airport to drive us over to East Manhattan. Our associate had worked with a professional men's league. The entire drive over he shared his wisdom while we listened intently. This was indeed exciting. We were told the ups and downs of working with professional athletes. We were told this was a great idea. We could make some money, but we had to remember women athletes weren't making much money in the states. Overseas the players were making an average of six figures. We could negotiate more in the way of fees and bonuses if we represented ladies who played in other countries. Our focus wasn't just on making money, we also wanted to be good role models and help create alternative paths for female athletes.

Now, as exciting as all this was, I was very concerned about how we were going to make all of the connections we needed. I was also concerned about how much money it was going to cost us up front to get our foot in the door. My partner was good with money.

She did a budget. Her estimate was over ten thousand dollars to start our company. Well, the room in Manhattan was $200 a night! We were already feeling the sting of this new business venture. (I had to remember *Everything Has A Price!*)

When we walked into the Marriott Hotel in East Manhattan, I thought, "Hmmm, this lifestyle might not be too bad!" The doorman greeted us with a warm hello and directed us to the check-in-counter. When we settled in the room, our first observation was, "This is nice, but boy are the rooms small in the Big Apple." As if we hadn't strategized enough, we took out our laptops and started working. Despite being in the big apple, we were very focused. We had to take the agent's exam when we returned home. Time was of the essence.

The next morning, we woke up with excitement. Today we would get to meet our competition. Agents from around the globe that represented women in the WNBA would all be gathered in one room. We got an early start. As we walked to the conference we were taking everything in. It was a chilly morning. We were stylish with our business suits and leather jackets. The streets were crowded. Despite the fact we thought we were walking fast, natives were zooming by us. We had our briefcases on our shoulders. This was a business trip that could launch us into our destiny.

We had thought about the possibilities. We had talked about the possibilities. Now we were actually living the vision. As we arrived in the registration area, we were greeted by a young lady from the Players Association I had spoken to many times. Being from the south, I greeted her with a huge hug. After all, I was just happy to be there! We picked up the registration packet before entering the conference room. We were among the first to arrive. We chose where we wanted to sit, took off our jackets and started introducing ourselves to the other agents.

We found most of the agents to be very friendly. We were networking like the pros. We exchanged cards, asked general questions like how long they had been an agent, or what type of clients they represented. When the meeting started we were both like sponges! We were absorbing everything! The meeting was very informative and helpful!

On the walk back to the hotel, we compared observations and information. We were definitely on to a great idea. They were approximately thirty agents in the meeting and less than half were women. We decided we were going to take over the women's sports arena. We would be so good; we would have to turn clients away! Once we were back in our room, we decided we would limit the number of players we would represent. This would allow us to give individual attention to each player. The magic number was fifteen. One of us would have seven players the other eight. We would both be available to the players, but based on each player's preference and how we interacted with them, each player would have a primary agent.

Next we mapped out how the office would work. When possible we would recruit together. We would both have access to the players' files, keeping detailed records of our interaction with the players. At any moment one of us should be able to pick up the players file and know exactly what the status of their contracts were, what the latest stats were in addition to having a listing of any marketing or speaking jobs they had been booked for. My partner would compile the statistics for each player. She would also be the chief contract negotiator. I would be their speech coach and public relations consultant. The plan was coming together nicely. We had figured out we probably wouldn't make any money the first year, but we were banking on the financial possibilities paying off.

When we returned home we hit the books hard studying for the exam. The exam was administered on a touch screen computer. My partner and I were in separate testing rooms. As I read through the questions, I was relieved I knew most of the information. I finished slightly before she did. I received my score within minutes of notifying the proctor. I had passed!

I waited for my partner in the lobby area. We celebrated with hugs as she announced she had passed the exam as well. We were one step closer to becoming sports agents. The possibility was quickly becoming a reality.

Six weeks later the State of Florida granted us our license. It was time to start pounding the pavement. How were we going to find our first clients? We had decided very early on we would ease our way into the field. We both had full-time jobs, so our goal was to be ready by the WNBA draft of 2000. This gave us about six months to work our plan.

Sometimes, when you have a plan, it will lead you to connectors when you least expect them. Armed with our agents' licenses, the 2000 Orlando Miracle season took on a whole new role in our lives. We were season ticket holders. At each game we would critique players, talk about our company and how successful we were going to be. Our initial connections with coaches and other agents had been a good start, but we needed a player. Ask and you shall receive! During the season, the team had a special practice for season ticket holders. My partner and I jumped on the opportunity to get up close and personal with the players. The practice session was fun to watch, but we wanted to get to the heart of why we where there. We wanted to start the question-and-answer session which would be held afterwards.

There were only about 100 people allowed in the special session which made it even better. People asked general questions about the team, the season or the players. My question was, "what did they do after the four month season?" I was curious for several reasons. First, I knew how much money they were making and second, I knew those who weren't playing overseas during the fall would be a good target for our sports agency. The answers varied from player to player. Some were playing overseas, some going back to school, some working in the States in various professions. However, the majority of the players would be playing overseas. The money was really good in other countries for female basketball players.

After the questions the players were available to take pictures with the season ticket holders. My partner and I decided to hang around upstairs in the lobby area after the session was over. Patience really is a virtue! Much to our delight, one of the players from the team who had an outstanding season came out to just mingle. She had an outstanding personality and was definitely one of the crowd favorites. She started greeting the fans who were hanging around. When she got to my partner and I, she asked us what we did for a living. Our guess was the suits made us stick out from the rest of the group. We answered enthusiastically stating we were lawyers who started a female sports agency. She told us to stick around for a minute she wanted to talk with us.

We waited patiently. We were so excited we could hardly contain it. My partner reminded me I had not wanted to wait originally. But see what happens when you follow your gut. Yes, she was right; the wait had paid off for us. When the player finished signing autographs she came over to speak with us. Her first question showed she was very intelligent and business-oriented. "What is going to make your agency different from the others?" She asked. We were ready! We responded by saying we were going to be a full-service agency offering public speaking, and image consulting in addition to helping the athletes become marketable in other professions. She spent a good fifteen to twenty minutes talking to us about female athletes and what they looked for in an agent. During the conversation we shared our backgrounds with her. She immediately asked me about the public speaking aspect of my career. She indicated she wanted to be a motivational speaker after her basketball career. At the conclusion of the conversation she asked us for our business cards and stated she would be in touch.

My partner and I had driven separate cars to the event. As soon as we where in the car, we were on our cell phones debriefing. Debriefing is what we called going over the day's events and if necessary, making decisions based on those events. We knew we had some decisions to make after meeting the Orlando Miracle player. First, we would not attempt to be her agent. Instead, we wanted to hear her views about agents. We wanted to run our ideas by her. She was the missing equation to all of these wonderful ideas we had. She could tell us what players were really looking for. She could provide a tremendous advantage for us. We both sent a short email to the player stating it was a pleasure meeting her and thanking her for her time. We received a short message back but for the rest of the season we did not hear from her.

One afternoon in the fall, I checked my voice mails and "surprise!" The player from the Orlando Miracle had left me a message. She wanted to talk with me about public speaking. I was eager to speak with her. First thing was first. I called my business partner to tell her the good news. Ok, let's back up, I told her what I thought would be good news. I learned very quickly we had left some major scenarios out in our original planning stages.

We had discussed how to charge for services my company, EHAP Inc. offered. In essence my position was the EHAP Inc. and I would be a subcontractor for certain services. One of those services would be speech coaching. The premise was simple, EHAP Inc. was a separate company. The entire focus of EHAP Inc. was public speaking and consulting. So if I offered these services as an agent I would be undercutting my existing company. My partner and I agreed we would contract my services through the sports agency. The sports agency would pay EHAP via an invoice system just like any other client. Sounds fair and straightforward right? Wrong!

As I told my partner the Miracle player wanted to meet for lunch. She was under the impression we were all going to lunch. Hmmm, this was an interesting situation. The player did not call about our sports agency. She called about speaking services offered through EHAP. So why would my partner take part in an initial meeting about my speaking services? In my mind this was a great opportunity for me to meet with her to talk about speaking services, then set up a date for my partner and I to meet with her to discuss the sports agency. My partner saw it differently... much differently! Her position was since we met the player at an event where we were technically representing the sports agency, the player should contract my services through the sports agency. Therefore she should be a part of this first meeting.

There are going to be times in your journey when you come to a crossroad. I think these times are crucial because they force you to go back to the basics. Remember when I told you about my vision in the beginning of the book? I didn't see me running around the country representing athletes. I didn't see me with a business partner changing the world of female athletics. What I saw was very clear. I saw me with books selling like crazy and speaking in front of massive audiences. So when my partner and I disagreed as to what would happen with my true talent which was speaking and speech consulting, my spirit became very clear. I could walk away because being a sports agent was not my dream, nor was it my calling.

Let me insert a word of caution here. I honestly believe you shouldn't give up on your dream at the first sign of trouble or during your first disagreement. I believe in working through complications to pursue your vision. The problem here was pursuing the sports agency was becoming a distraction from my dream. The enthusiasm I felt in the beginning was turning into a struggle between my company and the agency. I thought I had made myself perfectly clear. I didn't expect my partner to give up her law practice nor would I have anything to do with her practice. In turn, I wouldn't compromise EHAP Inc. and she would not have anything to do with EHAP. So you can imagine my surprise when out of the blue one day she told me she could assist with public speaking. How? This wasn't her background. Giving a speech or two doesn't qualify you to be a speech coach. I had very little civil background in the law. There was no way I would have suggested for her to let me assist her with a mediation issue. The lines were becoming crossed and it wasn't comfortable.

Once you start down the wrong path, it becomes easy to stay on the path because it is easier than getting off. Think about this. We had already sent out hundreds of announcements about our new sports agency. We had already invested thousands of dollars in start up costs. We had taken an exam. We had started passing out business cards. We had incorporated with the State of Florida. If I made the decision to walk away, people would think I was crazy. I would lose money I couldn't afford to lose. When I thought about the options I was still very clear that somehow, I had gotten on the wrong path. More importantly this path was taking me away from my dream, not bringing me closer to it. The real issue in my mind was does hanging in this partnership bring me any closer to my dream or will it cost me more in the long run?

I called my business partner to inform her I was going to walk away. At this point she wanted to have a conversation to explain why she felt the way she did. This is the example she gave me: If Michael Jordan who is one of the world's most famous male basketball players called her about a civil case she would automatically tell me about it because he was an athlete and we owned a sports agency. Ok, that makes sense right? But my question was would you accept the case through the sports agency when it has nothing to do with sports and you have a separate law firm that deals with civil matters? Her answer was yes, she would accept the fees through the sports agency. Then the agency would pay her law firm for the services. Ok, that sounds fair as well. But the issue is if Michael Jordan walked in your law firm and asked for legal representation would you tell him, I will only represent you if you go through my sports agency. We all know the answer to that question is no, she wouldn't. I have to add one other issue. It seemed to me there was a potential conflict of interest on the part of the player to contract with another sports agency for services when they already had a sports agent.

There are times when you must agree to disagree because the reality of the matter is no matter how much you discuss the issue you are not going to resolve it. This was one of those times for my partner and I. When I tried to balance out the pros and cons, there was one question I could not forget. If we disagree on something so fundamental, which is the very essence of my talents and my dreams, how could we make this work? As grim as it sounds, the truth was my partnership in the sports agency wouldn't work for several reasons.

First, there were small things which made big differences in our partnership. We had some differences of opinions when it came to style. I wanted to divide the labor so each of us would have clear duties and responsibilities. I don't work well on a continuous basis with collaboration projects. I am a team player but I'm also a very task-oriented person. When it comes to my talents I can be creative, but I need the freedom to do what I do best. Now add to the equation my lack of desire to get involved with what you are doing unless it is absolutely necessary or involves something I am working on. The result is I am a self-starter and work well alone.

On the other hand my partner liked the idea of collaboration. She liked doing almost everything together when it came to the sports agency. In the beginning what appeared to be a nice blend ended up being detrimental to our partnership. I knew I had to walk away. She could have the sports agency. I would pay the portion of outstanding debt I had helped secure. I didn't want to leave her stranded or holding the bag, but this was not my dream. I could not invest any more time or money in something that was clearly the wrong path for me.

Hindsight always reveals the truth in every matter. The truth in this situation was the sports agency was a short detour to introduce me to the world of sports. The Orlando Miracle player became my speaking client. She taught me a lot about sports in addition to how the sports arena worked. She connected me with several key contacts in the sports world. We worked on numerous speeches while forming a great relationship. I became her speaking manager. I signed another Orlando Miracle player. I was both a speaking coach and manager. The way I could merge sports and my dream was as a speaking coach not as an agent. As a speech coach, I didn't have to travel all over the country recruiting and scouting. As a speech coach I didn't have to worry about negotiating contracts for my clients. My job was simply to do what I know like the back of my hand: teaching them how to communicate effectively in public. What started out as me walking away from the world of sports really ended up being the beginning of a path in speaking and sports.

In the process I learned another great lesson: I don't want to manage people's dreams. My true desire is to encourage individuals to identify and live their dreams. It is important to make sure those individuals understand their dreams are going to come with a price. As a speech manager I started to see my clients were depending on me to make their dreams a reality. They wanted to make a certain amount of income during the off-season but they wanted me to make it a reality. The problem with this is no one can sell you better than you! No one knows you better than you! At times I found myself minimizing my marketing of EHAP and development in order to maximize my clients exposure.

When it is your vision, YOU must see it through. No one and I repeat no one can or will make your dream a reality if you don't believe in it with all of your heart and soul! On the other hand, you can't let someone else's dream steal you away from your vision. The players came up with an incredible idea to host an empowerment retreat for players in the WNBA. They explained the collective bargaining agreement would expire soon. This was going to be a key season of negotiation for the ladies. They needed to be inspired and empowered. The vision was huge but could be accomplished. I was excited. We set up a meeting to discuss how I could assist in making their vision a reality. It was decided I would coordinate the event and form a committee to assist with all of the details. The players were responsible for getting their colleagues to attend and help us get speakers in the industry.

We chose Walt Disney World as our host venue because of the beautiful resorts. The four theme parks would provide plenty of entertainment for our guests. We were not going to settle! This was going to be an outstanding event. We had the players in the WNBA complete a survey to assist us with the planning. The players listed numerous concerns. They wanted to improve their image, learn how to network, balance their stress, explore other career options and overcome the fear of public speaking to enter the field of professional speaking. The results of the survey were encouraging. We started the ground work. The committee was formed. The committee was a group of six women I had the utmost confidence in. It is imperative to surround yourself with people you can trust to get the job done.

We started booking speakers who were trailblazers in the Women's Basketball arena from around the country. Our program was coming together nicely. Our speakers were going to discuss image, career choices off the court, spiritual balance, domestic violence, public speaking, stress management, television opportunities and coaching careers. I was delighted when I met two African American Stunt Women from Hollywood, California who were going to talk about not being afraid to jump out of a window to pursue your dreams. The program would fill three mornings with workshops and end with a luncheon each day. The afternoons were open for the players to enjoy the theme parks. We packaged the program nicely in a professional brochure then mailed it to over two hundred players in the league. We needed fifty players for the event to be a success.

The players had the responsibility to make sure their teammates and colleagues in the league registered. Neither I nor the committee had those types of relationships to sell the retreat beyond the planning and presentation on paper. When you start to pursue your vision, the vision will always appear to be larger than you. The challenges become very apparent and can turn your dream into a nightmare. The challenge in this situation was financial sponsorship. This event was being planned after the September 11, 2001 attacks on the World Trade Centers in New York which not only killed thousands of people but had a tremendous affect on our economy. Many of our potential corporate sponsors had major budget cuts which didn't leave a lot of funds for charitable giving.

I find it amazing when people say, "Hey, I am ready to walk away from what might be a life changing experience because I don't have the resources or the know how to make my vision a reality. So I'll

let fear (which is really a lack of faith) rob me of my true destination." That is what happened with what would have been the first of its kind empowerment seminar for players of the WNBA. The players abandoned their vision because they were afraid we wouldn't have enough money. They were also offended the committee asked them to be accountable by reporting to us on their progress with getting players to register. When people leave their dream in your hands they demand your accountability, but when you challenge them about what they have been doing to make their dream a reality, they become offended. Absolutely amazing!

The committee being full of faith called a meeting immediately. The committee allowed them to speak first. The claimed a lack of knowledge caused them not to be able to explain the program to the players. For example, one of their teammates said they received the brochure. It was nice, but why was the registration so expensive? Another question was what's going to happen with the money. They claimed they couldn't respond because they didn't know. I immediately challenged this statement. Every meeting had an agenda and minutes. Every aspect of this event was explained to them on a constant basis. The registration fee was recommended by the players in the survey process. So this excuse was not valid. One player responded to the committee by saying, "Yes, I received stuff in the mail, but I didn't read it. I am not good at that kind of stuff. Whatever Veraunda said, I believed her because she is such a good business woman. I didn't think I had to worry about it." When I heard this I was saddened because when you put your future in someone's hand you give away all of your power.

I remembered a conversation with one of the players very early on. She said, when she does basketball camps, she just shows up, the people do all of the work. Before I could articulate this thought, the player told the committee, "As basketball players we are used to people doing everything for us. We just show up! We were trusting Veraunda along with the committee would make it happen and just tell us what we needed to do." Ok, that is fair. But this was not the committee's vision. This wasn't my vision; it was theirs. We were there to help facilitate the process. You can't have a vision, and believe it will just happen, then you can just show up! You have got to be willing to put in the work and go through the process. As basketball players I wondered what did their coach do? The coach didn't play the game for the team. The coach simply comes up with a plan which the players have to execute if they want to win the game!

The players abandoned their vision because they weren't sure they could get the players to register for the retreat. In essence, what they were saying is we don't know how to sell our vision. We came up with this great idea, but now we are being challenged to go beyond our comfort zone. We don't have faith that we can do it, therefore we aren't going to try. We'd rather lose the money we have invested. We aren't going to worry about our reputations or the amount of information that has been disseminated. We are just going to walk away. The committee and I were shocked.

I was furious in the beginning! How dare they walk away after we had done all of this work for them without any compensation! How dare they walk away after we put our name on thousands of letters and brochures! How dare they quit this project when they wouldn't dare quit in the middle of a basketball game just because they were behind on the scoreboard! This wasn't a game! This was an opportunity to establish themselves professionally as leaders and innovators in Women's Basketball. How dare they!

The committee brought me back to reality, "Veraunda, this was their vision. Let them walk away from their vision. It's time for the committee to regroup and continue to move forward." We as a committee asked ourselves a hard question: What did we learn from this experience? The answer was we definitely needed to continue with a new vision for the project. It was clear we needed to still have an empowerment seminar for female athletes but we needed to start with younger athletes. One of the committee members made a wonderful observation, "Veraunda, life is full of seasons, these players brought us together. We have formed a wonderful working relationship as well as great friendships. Their decision hasn't changed who we are as individuals or our mission as a committee. Our path hasn't changed. The players chose to go in another direction."

The committee decided to make some minor adjustments then keep straight ahead. This was not the time for us to walk away from what we believed in. This event was working for us. We had bought into the original vision. We wanted to pursue it.

You are probably wondering what happened to the relationships with my business partner in the sports agency and the players I consulted. When I walked away, I had no negative feelings towards my partner. However, we both pulled away and ceased our day-to-day interaction. There were a few outstanding items that had to be taken care of. We had very civil conversations about the remaining business. When I see her in public I feel comfortable talking to her. I sincerely wish her success in all of her endeavors. My walking away didn't change her vision. She continued with the sports agency. Let's be clear, there was no need for my walking away to change her destination if in fact working with female athletes was her passion and her dream. With or without me, her vision could become a reality. There is no need for you to take transitions personally. Life is full of transitions. The way you deal with them will shape your character and teach you how to be resilient.

The relationship with the players turned out a little differently. One of the players alleged my business decision to recover my costs by deducting them from her speaking income was theft. Needless to say that conversation was not pleasant. I withdrew my representation of her as her speaking manager and speech coach immediately. Again, there was no need for ill feelings. Business is business! No need to stay on a path that was not productive or positive.

The other player did pay her invoice for outstanding costs. My hope was to maintain a relationship with her because we had started to form a great friendship. She had tremendous potential as a speaker and as a business woman. She had a warm spirit and was generally open to new ideas. I really enjoyed working with her. However, she had an attorney send me a letter requesting no further contact in addition to stating she had no intention of paying any damages assessed as a result of the decision to cancel the retreat. I had to honor this request. As unfortunate as it was, I also had to move on with some key business decisions. I could only hope for the season I was a part of her life was positive and productive. She had definitely been a positive influence in mine.

The cancellation of the empowerment retreat caused a breach of contract with the host facility which resulted in over $36,000 in damages for my company. I made the decision to file a civil law suit to recover the damages. If you decide to own a business, there are prices to pay. The players' decision to walk away shouldn't have cost me. But it did. I was dissapointed, but learned a valuable lesson.

At times when you are pursuing your dream you will feel like saying, "I don't know why I bother to buy into other people's dreams. I don't know why I care." You feel like you have been suckered into a feel-good moment which turns into a nightmare. Have you ever heard the statement, "It's how you look at the glass that will make the difference?" In my case, I reminded myself the glass was half full. I learned invaluable business and personal lessons through my experiences in the world of female sports. I formed great relationships which are still flourishing. I was exposed to various situations which provided me an opportunity to decide what I enjoy doing and what I have no interest in pursuing. These experiences were all a part of the journey. They helped guide me back to my true path which is speaking, writing and consulting! That is my core!

Prior to finishing this chapter, RDV Sports and the WNBA announced the Orlando Miracle would not be returning to Orlando for the 2003 season. The management company for the Orlando Miracle decided they were losing too much money. It was time for the company to walk away. The WNBA made a decision they would relocate the team to another city. I, along with many others had anticipated the move because of a drop in attendance over several seasons. The decision was not received well by many people. Many fans hated to see the team leave. On the other hand many in the Central Florida area said they could care less. Others were happy to see the team go. Just another reminder you have to be true to YOUR core. Sometimes what the crowd says can confuse you in addition to costing you. The bottom line for the RDV Sports Company was they didn't have the support of enough people to make the team work in Orlando.

As I read the newspapers, it became clear to me, every day people who are successful have to make difficult decisions. One of the hardest decisions is whether or not they should walk away from something they thought they wanted or believed in. The Chief Officer for the RDV Sports organizations said it wonderfully, "We believe strongly in the WNBA product and think it will continue to succeed in other markets. Unfortunately, we were not able to make it work financially in Orlando. We feel it is time to focus all of our resources on our core product – the Orlando Magic."

A few weeks later a friend called me to report the ownership for the Miami Heat had decided not to renew or buy their WNBA Miami Sol team. This decision meant Florida would not have anymore WNBA teams. I immediately went to the website to see why the Heat organization made this decision. The spokesperson said, "We have greatly enjoyed our WNBA experience, especially our relationships with our players and fans, and continue to believe the women's pro game has a bright future, but our plans are to redirect our energies to our other business interests." Once again, a business decision was being made to refocus. What I find interesting is in refocusing a decision was made to walk away from one interest or product to pursue or maximize another interest or product.

When you are pursuing your dream you must stay true to your core product. There are times when I get really excited about ideas. When I look at the possibilities I always have to ask myself: "Is this idea or opportunity going to help me develop or enhance my core product?" Sometimes, I don't know the answer to the question until I try. I walk down the path a little bit and depending on what happens I keep going, turn around or walk away.

Do you know what your core products are? In my case they are my ability to speak and write to empower others on their journey through life. I can't venture too far away from those two basic products. When an opportunity arises now, I try to evaluate the short-term and long-term benefits to me, to EHAP Inc. in addition to the other parties involved. Depending on the outcome of the analysis, I have to make a decision. There is no right or wrong answer as to when you should try something new. You never know when it will pay off. You also never know when it will backfire miserably. Nothing beats a failure but a try! If a farmer never planted seeds because he was trying to figure out what type of season it was going to be, he would guarantee his demise. There would be no harvest season, because there had not been any planting of seeds to yield a crop.

If you try one path and it doesn't work out, try again if you can identify what you can do differently to make it work. If you figure out in the middle of the journey it is not for you or it is taking you away from your core, change your direction. Walking away isn't failure it is simply changing your direction. Depending on the situation you might need to run to get away as fast as you can to minimize your losses!

There is no need to harbor ill feelings. If it doesn't work, it doesn't work. It is just that simple! Wish those who weren't meant to travel the entire journey with you well in their future endeavors. Give thanks for what they brought into your life for the season they were an asset. Then pick up the pieces and keep moving.

Don't let other people deflate your dream. Don't let other people pull you on to paths you shouldn't be on. Just because they give up doesn't mean you are supposed to give up. If you get off track, regroup, refocus and get back to the main highway as soon as you can. When you are driving to a predetermined destination you usually use a map. Every once and a while, in the middle of a trip you miss an exit or take a short cut that proves to be wrong. Some people drive around lost for long periods of time too stubborn or proud to stop and ask for help. Despite being lost, we rationalize driving around aimlessly by saying sooner or later we will figure it out. The problem is while we are riding around lost, we are wasting gas and valuable time.

When you are following your destiny, time and energy are very valuable. If you get off the path you run the risk of losing sight of the core product. You run the risk of becoming tired, frustrated and losing the ability to get back on the main highway. You also run the risk of just giving up because of the stress and frustration which often accompanies being lost. Whatever the situation, you must stay true to your core product and be smart enough to know when to walk away! Sometimes others will need to walk away from you. It's o.k., let them go. I can't emphasize how important it is to wish them well and be thankful for the time you traveled together. Spending time or energy on negative thoughts or interaction with them is a complete waste and has no positive impact on your journey!

Hmmm, trying to figure out when you should stay and when you should go is really hard. Figuring out which direction you should go can also be challenging. When you decide to make your vision a reality there is one thing that very few people will tell you. Seeing the huge vision is just the beginning. Making it a reality is a difficult journey. How to get to your destination is never clear in the vision.

The vision is designed to keep you focused and motivated on the journey. The vision is the voice that keeps whispering, "Don't give up, keep going, you can do it!" The vision is also what steers you back on the right path when you get lost. The voice of the vision might be telling you to stop and stand still. In my case, my vision was not of me at basketball games recruiting, it wasn't me flying around the country negotiating contracts, it wasn't me fighting with other people about their visions. My vision was clear, I would be traveling the world speaking to huge audiences and writing books. My vision reminded me I couldn't give up, instead I had to refocus my energies on my core products. My vision whispered, "Veraunda, it is imperative for you to know when to move full speed ahead, when to be still, and when to walk away!" Your vision will become your voice guiding you throughout your journey. Your challenge is hearing the voice and obeying it!

Apply the lesson in this chapter to your life:

What situations in your life do you need to walk away from and why?

What situations are you staying in because it seems easier than starting over?

When you go back to your core, what is most important to you?

What does "No" really mean?

Everyone has heard the phrase, "No means No!" Our parents use it when they are trying to get us to stop asking them for something we want. They use words like, "Didn't I tell you no, already? Why are you asking me again?" Our bosses say it when we are trying to obtain a new office or a raise. "The budget hasn't changed since we discussed the raise three months ago. I'm sorry, I can't offer you more money or buy you new office furniture." Even our significant others say it, "We've discussed this issue before and I haven't changed my mind since the last conversation!" Regardless of the words used, what each of these scenarios say very clearly is "No! means No!"

About three years into my entrepeneurship experience, I was forced to question what "No!" really means. During the third year, I became frustrated with the process of owning a business. I grew tired of living from paycheck to paycheck. One month could be awesome with the next month being a struggle. I had read some great financial books that helped me devise what I thought was a great plan to eliminate my financial debt. I read about an intriguing new term. Linear income is what the financing industry calls a steady paycheck from a "job." The theory behind linear income is very simple, once you have a steady pay check, you create a plan to pay certain household bills with your paycheck, then you find other streams of income to pay off your debt. Let me give you an example of how this would work:

I listed every credit card bill I had in one column on a sheet of paper. In another column I listed all of my monthly household expenses. Finally, I listed things I would like to be able to do every month as extras in a third column. When I totaled each column at the end of the page, the numbers provided some vital information. The first column was my debt I wanted to eliminate. It was quite a bit of money. The second column was what I had to bring in each month to make ends meet. The third column showed me what I would have clear to be able to splurge a little each month. To really keep my head above water, I had to add column one and two. My credit debt plus my monthly household expenses was the minimum I had to earn to get through a month. The problem was some months EHAP Inc. would make double the amount I needed at other times it would only make half of what I needed.

After three years of up and down, I was very aggravated! I had temped. I had prayed. I had worked under a contract for a steady entity almost an entire year. I had taught part-time. I had done everything I could think of other than go back to work full-time. I had been faithful to the vision of EHAP Inc. But what happens when everything you own is on the line every month? What happens when the bill collectors keep calling? You can't explain to them you have this vision you are working towards that will take a little time to make a reality. What happens when you decide you can't live like this anymore???

I got desperate! I became afraid. Keisha started to talk to me:

Keisha: *Veraunda, it has been three years! We aren't any better off than when we started. Do you realize we could have paid off all of our debt by now? If you had continued to work for the government you could have done your speaking on the weekend, using all of that money to pay off our debt. We have lost three years! You have to do something now. Let's start looking for a job! It doesn't have to be for five years, but just long enough for you to get back on solid ground. You will have benefits; you can complete the one year you need to vest with the State of Florida, not to mention you can have peace of mind. Every month we are trying to figure out how we are going to make it. Every month we are hoping the checks from clients will arrive on time. This is getting old! This isn't what you saw in the vision Veraunda!*

Lucy: *Well, let's slow down for a minute. You have to look at it from another perspective Veraunda. You have never had your lights turned off. You are* *still living in your home. You still have your car. You have never been seriously ill. You are still eating. You have even been able to purchase new items and go to the hair salon. Keisha is making it sound worse than it really is. Even on our worst day, we have still been blessed. So the question becomes how will going back to work full-time fit into your Creator's plan for you?*

Keisha: Look, I am not saying God has not been faithful, all I am saying is it has been really hard for us. I don't believe God made us to struggle like this. Haven't you ever heard God helps those who help themselves? So I am making a simple suggestion that we help ourselves by going to work like the rest of America does everyday!

I had to seriously think about Keisha's point. Millions of people go to work every day to pay their debt, so why was I any different? Lucy jumped in before I could finish figuring it out.

*Lucy: Veraunda don't you dare let Keisha fool you. You work everyday! You work harder now than when you were an attorney. You work from sun up to sun down. When you temp, you give an office eight hours then you come home and work until midnight. You work on weekends. Don't let Keisha minimize your efforts for your company. This is work! There are millions of people who own small companies that are working just like you are to make ends meet. They are facing the same challenges you are facing. They work long hours hoping that clients will pay on time. They are a one-stop shop just like you. They are the receptionist, the office assistant, marketing representative and the product all wrapped up in one package. It's OK, Veraunda. You are not alone and you **WILL** make it!*

Keisha: Lucy, it is great to be a cheerleader! It is super you are so analytical. My question is what are we going to do if we lose this house? What are we going to do if the car is picked up because we couldn't make the payments? What are we going to do if we get seriously sick? What are we going to do??? Things are really bad! It would be different if this was our first year in business, but it is our third! Maybe, just maybe, God wants us to go back to work. What about that idea Lucy? It's not the end of the world! In fact we would be better off down the road. Veraunda can get some more legal experience in the civil arena,

---

which would help us with EHAP Inc. She could pay off all of her credit debt in a year and a half, so if she finds a job for two years we will be debt free and have some money in the savings account. We will continue to develop EHAP, but we will only speak on weekends or limited big events using our vacation time during the week. When EHAP is able to pay all of our household and company expenses then we will resign to try EHAP full-time again. However, we need to do something differently to get out of this financial sinkhole. It just keeps getting bigger and bigger!

Lucy: Now wait a minute! That is not true! Veraunda, what about the time you thought you were going to have to turn your cell phone off? You called the company to terminate the service and the woman gave you a special cutting your bill in half in addition provided you with double the minutes. What about the time when you had to make a decision about trying to purchase your car after leasing it for three years? You had no money to put down. Your credit seemed very shaky. You kept avoiding the calls from the company asking you what you would like to do with the car. Finally one month before a decision had to be made; you received a call from a nice male representative of the car company. You explained the situation to him and he encouraged you to just try to purchase the car. He said he could do it over the phone by asking you a few simple questions. You answered them and your miracle happened within minutes! You were approved to transfer the lease into a purchase. That was over two years ago! You were scared and worried for absolutely no reason other than Keisha coming up with all these problems that God has always solved for you! There are many more examples of how your needs have always been met. So let's not panic here.

Keisha: I am not suggesting we panic. I am suggesting we go to work for two years to help ourselves out of all this financial debt.

Keisha made sense. I understood what Lucy was saying, but Keisha seemed more logical at the time. I could work two years without blinking. I wrote a plan because Keisha was absolutely right. I could pay off all my credit card debt, save some money, have great benefits, and finish vesting with the government. It started sounding better the more I thought about it. Keisha was on to something here. I even figured out how I could keep speaking, writing and consulting without jeopardizing a full-time job. The beauty of the plan was every dollar I made from EHAP, I could use to pay off a bill. It was sounding better by the minute!

Lucy: Veraunda, I have one simple question for you: are you being true to yourself by going back to work? Did you step out of the boat, just to get back in when the waters got rough? If you are honest, this crap Keisha is talking about only appeals to you because you want comfort and stability!

Keisha: Lucy, you are silly! Sometimes I think you are just outright crazy! When Peter stepped out the boat, Jesus didn't tell him to stay out on the water for the rest of his life. He stepped out, almost drowned, Jesus saved him and that was the end of the story. In the next chapter, Peter, along with Jesus and all the other disciples are back on land somewhere moving on with their lives. We have been stuck in the water for three years, crying out to Jesus to save us. And before you say one word, I know we haven't drowned, but we sure are close! We are tired! If we don't do something soon, we are going to be killed by the storms of financial debt!

Lucy: How many times did the situation look hopeless in the Bible? How many miracles were performed when it appeared it was over? How many successful people have been on the verge of giving up? How many times were they rejected when all of a sudden, someone loved their performance or idea? All it takes for us to get out of this situation is one word, one client, or one contract. We are not going to drown! Failure is not an option! Veraunda, this is just apart of the process. Be patient and be still!

Keisha: VERAUNDA, I'M SICK AND TIRED OF BEING SICK AND TIRED! (Fannie Lou Hammer said this in a plea for equal rights many years ago, now here we were using her words to describe our own struggle for survival.) Either you take action to change this situation or be ready to drown! You aren't giving up, you are refusing to sit back and let the storm suck you under. You are going to swim to the nearest boat, get in and go back to shore! There is nothing wrong with that. I am sick of Lucy and her foolishness. How can you inspire others while barely having enough to make it from day to day? That's crazy! Get your finances together Veraunda, then we can REALLY make a difference!

Keisha had another excellent point. There had been so many times when I had gone to speak with just a hope and prayer. There had been so many times when I wanted to give freely, but didn't have the money to do it. If I went back to a full-time job, I would be able to do more for those in need. Keisha was making more sense by the minute.

Lucy: Veraunda, please listen to me. What people need is for you to stay focused. People need you to share the messages from your heart. People need you to keep speaking and writing. People need you to be an example of perseverance. People need you to find the strength to survive which is what you told them to do in your first book. People need you to be willing to pay the price Veraunda!

Keisha: No, Lucy! You are wrong! She can't give what she doesn't have! Veraunda, people need you to be able to pay your bills. When people are paying your bills through your writing and your speaking that is when you focus on them. Right now, your focus in on surviving. You aren't abandoning the people; you are restructuring your position. Lucy's words of encouragement and positive thinking are nice, but they aren't enough to keep us from being eaten alive by the bills! Now that is the truth!

I had heard Keisha and Lucy pulling at me for over three years. I had tried everything I could to keep from "giving up" on EHAP. I agreed with Keisha, it was time for me to go find a real job. I rationalized the situation by trying to balance my life. I needed a more stable income. I was in a lot of debt. EHAP wasn't able to provide the financial stability I was looking for in the short term. Going back to work just seemed to make sense. No need to wait for the bills to consume me. I needed to take control of the situation. That is where the journey with "NO" begins!

In the process of a year I applied for three different jobs I thought would be absolutely wonderful. I never sought out the jobs. It seemed like the jobs found me. The first was a great opportunity to serve as the legal advisor for a local government entity. I was approached about the job by the second in command of the agency. I was honored. Starting salary $70,000!!! I was excited! I could pay off my debt within a year! I forwarded my resume immediately. I was scheduled for an interview within a matter of days.

I put on one of my conservative suits for the interview. I did my research on the agency so I would be prepared for the questions. But I must be honest; something in my spirit didn't want to go back to work full-time. I knew I would be going back to the rat race of long hours, lots of files on my desk, in addition to constant phone calls. Keisha reminded me why I was considering the position:

Keisha: *Girl, this would be perfect for us! Do you know what we can do with a $70,000 salary? All of our benefits are paid for including memberships in all of the legal bar associations! You will vest in a year. Anything over that will be absolutely free money! This is exactly what we need to get out of our financial storm! This is a wonderful opportunity!*

Lucy: *Yes, it is great money, but what about your vision? How will you find time to cultivate EHAP Inc.?*

Keisha: *Here she goes with that foolishness! We aren't going back over that again. It is just a short adjustment period. We are applying. We are interviewing. We will worry about what to do with EHAP once we know whether we get the job. But EHAP will be fine. Veraunda don't worry about the company, just go for the full-time job!*

The interview went very well. There were four people from various departments involved in the interview. They had narrowed it down to three final candidates. The job required 40-60 hours a week. I would be required to wear a pager so I could be reached for legal advice whenever needed. I would have three weeks of vacation. The agency would attempt to work with my schedule to allow speaking engagements as long as it was not interfering with my work. Several of the individuals in the interview mentioned they had heard wonderful things about my speaking. But one person sent chills through me when he asked, "One day you are going to be famous, why would you want to work here?" He saw the vision! I hadn't shared the vision with any of them, yet he saw it! As I walked out of the room, he said to me, "Veraunda, seriously think about the job. I took a promotion to become the head of this department. I really thought I wanted the promotion. I received a nice raise, but now I am stuck in my office all day. I miss the interaction with people I once had. Just think about it." Things aren't always what they appear to be.

I did think about it, but I still wanted the job. I wanted the security of the job. I wanted the salary! I could do the job! I knew I could balance EHAP and the job. As hard as I tried to convince myself there was still a voice speaking to me very quietly in a wise state of calm:

Lucy: *Veraunda, this is a great opportunity, but you are not really being true to yourself or to your vision. Do you want to work 40-60 hours a week? Do you really want to wear a pager all the time to take legal questions? Do you want to work in an office all day? Do you want to have files stacked up on your desk? Don't respond, just think about it.*

I thought about it. I convinced myself I could do it! I convinced myself I would do it! I waited patiently for the call saying I had gotten the job! But when the call came in a week later, it was a "No." The director of human resources called me from his cell phone to thank me for my interest in the position. However, they really needed someone with more employment law experience. They had chosen another candidate. However, he wished me well in all of my other endeavors. He was sure I would be successful. I wasn't sure how to feel. I was disappointed but in an odd way I also felt relief. In this case, I believed the "No" meant next.

There was another position I really wanted. I thought this position would be "better." It would still allow me to vest with the government but would also allow me to interact more with people while still making a difference. However, after submitting my resume for the position and speaking with the director nothing happened. There was never any clear direction on whether I would be hired for a full time position. This time instead of being disappointed, I realized I was being told "No" for a reason. The entity was having inner struggles that would have made it a very difficult environment to work in. Slowly, the "Nos" were beginning to push me towards my destiny.

It didn't take long for the next opportunity to present itself. A colleague told me about a position with another governmental agency providing an opportunity to advocate for children. I got excited just thinking about it. I was familiar with the law regarding children in the State of Florida. I would have a great salary, great benefits and be able to vest. This was definitely a good opportunity. I checked the monthly newspaper published by the Florida Bar Association. Much to my delight, the employment section listed the position with a great starting salary. I knew this was the right job! I took the ad in the newspaper as a sign I was on the right track. I immediately submitted my resume for the position. Two days after mailing the resume I received an email from the hiring chair. My heart was beating as I read the words, "I was impressed with your resume. We would love to schedule an interview as soon as possible."

No need to delay! I called immediately! The hiring chair was not available, but I left my cell phone number with his assistant. I was sitting in the dentist's office when I received the call. We had a very pleasant conversation. We knew a lot of the same people. It was a great start. We scheduled the interview for two weeks down the road. I knew several attorneys who worked for the department. I asked them to put in a good word for me.

The interview went well. I left feeling very comfortable I would receive a call offering me the position. Instead, there was "No" word about the job offer for weeks. When I finally followed up, I learned there was a hiring freeze statewide. I was shocked. The department was having some budget issues. Hmmm, another "No."

I became still at this point. I was not going to apply for anything else! I had been working since I was fourteen. I could not remember one time in my professional life when I interviewed for a job that I did not eventually receive an offer of employment. So what was going on?

Lucy: Girl, our Creator is trying to tell you something. These jobs do not fit into His plan for you. If it was His will for you to receive the jobs, it would have happened with ease. You are obviously a great asset to any company. But not every company fits in with your vision. This is almost funny. You continue to try to control your own destiny instead of walking in your purpose. Be still, Veraunda.

Keisha: *I don't see anything that is funny! I don't believe it is in our destiny to stay in financial stress. I don't believe our purpose is to let our law degree sit by silently while we are struggling every month to pay the bills. So my suggestion is to keep applying for positions until we get hired! Veraunda, please consider going back to the State Attorney's Office. You loved that job. You miss practicing. Just call!*

Lucy: *Veraunda be still. You are being told "No" for a reason.*

Keisha: *Oh, so now you are a psychic? If you know so much, then tell us why we are short on money. Tell us what we are supposed to do to get out of this debt.*

Lucy: *No, I am not a psychic. But I do know the Bible we read says, "I have NEVER seen the righteous forsaken nor His seed begging bread". I also know the 23rd Psalm says, "The Lord is my Shepherd and I shall not want!"*

Keisha: *This is not the time for a sermon. We don't need a sermon nor do we want a sermon! We want money to pay these bills! We want to get rid of this debt! We want financial freedom!*

Lucy: *All of those things will come with time. This is just a test to prepare us for the next level. When you have done all you know to do you should be still. The answer will appear. Sometimes when you get overwhelmed, the fear prevents you from thinking clearly. You become distracted. You can't focus on the vision. There will be a day when you won't have to worry about any of this. Just be patient.*

Keisha: *The vision did not include living from month to month. The vision did not include the challenges we are facing now! So what are we supposed to do? Sit here with all this education doing nothing? Are you crazy?*

Lucy: I go back to the Bible for the last word. "Be still and know that I am God."

Keisha: Veraunda you can be still and starve!

OK...enough is enough! By this time I had received three "Nos." They were all valid "Nos." Nonetheless, my financial situation had not improved. I was a bit confused about my next move. Should I keep applying for positions? Why was I being told "No?" Was there something better for me? Or was I being told "No" because EHAP Inc. had to remain a priority? I couldn't afford to be still. But I didn't know where to go. I wasn't sure what kind of job I really wanted. I wanted some flexibility in my schedule. I definitely didn't want to have to wear a suit and heels every day. But I wasn't afraid to work. I certainly didn't want to just wait and see what would happen. The situation was becoming complex. Every possibility seemed to be a dead end.

On the surface the situation did not seem to be improving but I must share with you that in reality miracles were happening every day. My lights had never been turned off. I was eating every day. Money always seemed to appear when I needed it. I was still speaking on a regular basis. EHAP was doing well by all standards. I lost sight of this fact because of the voice in my head that was screaming for stability and comfort. I wasn't walking in abundance but I wasn't walking in poverty by a long shot. When things seem like they are not working for you, you must go back to the basics.

I started receiving my answer in odd places. A good friend gave me a book entitled, "The Power of Now!" The book provided me with a much needed message. The author, Eckert Tolle, made a bold statement, "Everything you need at this moment, you have." I pondered the statement. He was right. I wasn't lacking anything at the moment. I was worried about the future. However, every day was miraculously taken care of.

Another friend recommended I read the "Seven Spiritual Laws of Success" by Deepak Chopra. I just started reading all kinds of books. When life gets rough, sometimes you have to hit the books! When the voices in your head are confusing you, find a way to seek your truth. Start feeding your spirit. My reading list was extensive but here are a few books that made a tremendous difference during my series of "Nos":

The Purpose Driven Life – Rick Warren
Feel the Fear and Do It Anyway – Dr. Susan Jeffers
The Four Agreements – Don Miguel Ruiz
Seven Spiritual Laws of Success - Deepak Chopra
The Power of Now – Eckert Tolle

I was building my mental strength. Just when you think you are grounded and have figured it out, the next dilemma shows up. When the next "opportunity" knocked at my financial door I was in a stable position financially. I wasn't "looking for a job." But this job sounded too good to be true!

A colleague told me about a marvelous opportunity to teach full-time at a local college. I immediately became excited because this had to be the answer I was looking for. There was a great salary, full benefits and I would be in the state retirement system. The best part of the deal was as a full time professor you only work ten months out of the year with optional summer contracts. This was it! This was perfect. I went online to look at the class schedule. Much to my pleasure, there were no Friday classes. This translated into flexibility to me. I could travel all I wanted on the weekends to speak with EHAP Inc. During the summer I could travel as much as I liked. This job appeared to be the perfect match to blend my speaking career with a steady job.

I started getting prepared for the interview. I submitted my resume' immediately. I started brushing up on my civil law. I was "studying" everyday. I was sure this was MY job. When I looked at the job description, I fit all but one area. I had not been a director of a program. However, I had taught for almost eight years. My student evaluations were usually very good. I believed the evaluations would have to be a positive factor. Once again, I had great letters of recommendation to support my application.

I progressed to stage one, which was a telephone interview. I was excited when I advanced to the onsite interview. There was a three-month delay, but I was sure the delay would work in my favor. On the day of the interview, I was ready. I was going to be the first candidate to interview for the position. I had a professional presentation ready for all eight members of the committee. I was comfortable with the questions. I had fun in the teaching portion of the interview. The committee seemed to enjoy themselves just as much as I did while answering questions about my hypothetical negligence lawsuit caused by a trucker with bad brakes. I had been creative with the factual scenario. I had a question for each committee member to illustrate my inclusive teaching method. Despite only two members of the committee having a law degree, everyone answered their question correctly. This quick grasp of negligence law based on my teaching was surely what the committee needed to confirm I would be a great addition to their already successful program. As I left, I believed I had set the standard for the remainder of the candidates. I had no idea what the other candidates brought to the table, but I was positive I would give them a solid challenge.

Imagine my dismay two days later when the dean of the program called to inform me I had not been chosen as one of the final two candidates. I told her thank you for a wonderful interview while trying to hold back the tears.

What was I going to do now? If this were not the perfect job, what would be? I felt like giving up! I was confused and disappointed. I have never been rejected so many times in my life. Before starting EHAP, every job I applied for I eventually was hired. Every goal I set, I reached. So my question was why were all of these doors being closed? What did this series of "Nos" really mean? It appeared I was stuck. I was forced to be still. Keisha tried to talk to me but Lucy immediately cut her off:

Lucy: Don't you dare fall into this pit. Everything happens for a reason. Veraunda if you are honest with yourself, you knew this wasn't the opportunity for you. You are not going to be able to do anything that takes you away from your mission to make a difference through EHAP. The doors are closing to keep you from making a huge mistake! The doors are closing to keep you from giving in to the pressure. Pay attention. It is about you staying focused on what you know you are destined to do. It is about YOU refusing to settle. Because you are under all of this pressure you are growing weak. The doors are closing to make you strong again.

The next major resource was a book that accompanied the last "No." A client recommended I read, "Feel the fear and do it anyway!" by Dr. Susan Jeffers. When my client recommended the book I thought, nice title, but I don't have a fear problem. I have a lot of pressure problems, which is very different. The first chapter of the book says, no matter what happens to us, we can handle it. Once I read those words I knew this book was a part of the voice whispering to me to stay on the path. I was beginning to believe the only way I could keep my head above water and pay off my debt was to return to a traditional job. The remainder of the book was just as timely as the first chapter because it reminded me when you want different results, you must try different things. Instead of going back to what was comfortable, it was time for me to get creative. The book was feeding my spirit during what I now refer to as a time of transition.

The Nos were helping me make the transition into a wonderful place. The thought that makes a difference for July of 2003 read as follows:

What does "NO" REALLY mean?

Have you ever experienced a series of the word "No" in your life? Let me explain what I mean by a series. You think you are ready for a promotion but you get a NO. You think you have found the right person for a lasting relationship but you find out in the middle of the relationship that it's a NO go! You apply for credit but the response is NO. Do you know what it feels like when you are trying to get out of a tough spot and all of the doors of opportunity appear to slam right in your face? I must be totally honest. This month, I have been experiencing a series of the word NO. I had made up my mind that in order to eliminate my debt I was going back to work this year. Come hell or high water, by August I was going back to using my law degree in some way to get ahead of the financial debt. In fact, I figured it out down to the dollar. If I worked for one full year I could pay off almost all of my debt. Anything beyond that would be gravy! I was excited, and applied for several great positions. But there was one small dilemma...what would happen to EHAP Inc.? The answer was simple... I would not abandon EHAP Inc....I would just cut back tremendously on my speaking. The answer to my solution was a resounding NO! I applied for four positions this year, all of which I thought were perfect fits for me. They were great opportunities to learn. They were positions I believed would allow me to make a difference in the lives of others and yet every single door was closed. Two "Nos" were because they wanted a different type of legal experience than I had. Another NO was because of budget cuts, and one no was NO openings in Central Florida at the time. I wondered what was going on here??? I know the economy is in a slump, but Lord have mercy...so was I!!! I had a plan and it wasn't working! This past weekend, I went back to my vision for EHAP Inc. I revisited why I left my job practicing law in the first place. It was to make a difference in lives across the country. I left practicing because I had a tremendous vision and needed the flexibility to travel. In my mind, I have had a great ride for three and a half years. I have enjoyed meeting you, speaking to you, writing for you. Now that the economy is in such a state of chaos I figured I needed to go back to a stable environment. (I wanted to be safe... so let me go back to what I know and I'll return to the vision once things are more stable.) However, this is not my Creator's plan for me. The "Nos" in my life have been signs I was trying to get off my divine path. God is not allowing me to mess up my life. So what does no mean? NO means NEXT! NO means NOT YET! NO means NOT THIS! NO means BE STILL! No means YOU CAN'T GIVE UP ON YOUR DREAM! NO means THE BEST IS YET TO COME!

I stand firmly by my belief angels always appear when you least expect them! A few weeks before my interview with the college I had received a call from one of my sorority sisters inquiring about whether I conducted training workshops for companies and governmental agencies. Why, of course I did! But no one knew this because I had marketed myself as a keynote speaker. My brain started working overtime. I forwarded her a list of my training sessions. I immediately heard Lucy come up with a terrific idea:

Lucy: Veraunda, you need to revisit your marketing ideas and your business plan.

Keisha: For what? Word of mouth has worked just fine. Not to mention we are not marketing specialists, nor do we have the money to hire a marketing firm.

Lucy: Thank you for pointing out our challenges.

Keisha: It's my pleasure. I'm just keeping it real!

Lucy: Anyway, as I was saying, Veraunda you just received a major yes in the midst of all these "Nos". What if you revisited your business plan to see how training would fit in? What if you designed a comprehensive workshop series for corporations and governmental agencies that would promote you as a trainer in addition to a keynote speaker? As a trainer, you will open the doors for revolving opportunities. As a keynote speaker you are limiting yourself to once-a-year events. Nothing wrong with opening or closing a conference, but what if you could build people all year long?

At that moment, the words popped into my head, "If you want to build your business, start with building your people!" I immediately jumped on the computer to create the program. I had a draft in less than a week. I sent a draft to my sorority sister who had inquired about my training services. I asked for her feedback. Did she think this was a program that companies needed? For the first time in a year, I received a resounding "YES!" She shared it with another department head who said he had no idea I covered the range of topics included in the program. In fact, their company had been discussing how to implement a comprehensive training program for the past year with no real solutions.

They were so excited about my program they asked me if I could produce enough copies for each department manager. Within two days I forwarded eighty proposals to various departments. Imagine my surprise and delight when I received a phone call two days later from a department telling me my program is exactly what they had been looking for! By the week's end, I had secured a major training contract that was the largest lump sum of fees I had ever booked. This was just one department! One idea during my series of "Nos" created a major opportunity. However, the doors were starting to open in various venues.

If there is one thing I would say to you about your journey when you are facing challenges, I would say be persistent! When one door closes, knock on another door. Eventually you will find the right one that allows you to explore your true passion and live in your infinite possibilities. Within two weeks of the door closing at the college, I had received a contract that would allow me to make significant progress in my financial debt. I could see how things were beginning to come together not only for my personal journey, but also for my professional career.

Once, I created the training program, other programs just started coming to me faster than I could create them. Ideas would keep me up at night until I wrote them down to make sure I didn't forget them. Another angel appeared via email. There is a young man I met through a professional organization of black journalists. When he received my "Thought that makes a difference," about the "Nos" he emailed me to set up a phone conference. He lives in Chicago, I have only met him once in three years when he showed up at a workshop I was doing on public speaking. Mr. Landry is an exceptional person. For some unknown reason, he had taken a serious interest in my success. Periodically, he would send me newspaper articles with ideas of how I could expand my business. But this particular time, he wanted to talk to me. It proved to be another tremendous door opening. His first suggestion to me had been about a year earlier:

In 2001, Mr. Landry had recommended I submit my materials to the SAFE conference, which deals with the issues of Sexual Assault and Domestic Violence on college campuses. I was hesitant to do so because I wasn't sure I wanted to work in this very difficult field. As a prosecutor I had found the Sex Crimes and Domestic Violence work very rewarding because of the ability to make a difference in the lives of my victims. My question was, what would I speak to professionals in the sex crime arena about? The title of my presentation came to me so quickly it scared me! It was simple and self-explanatory:

Lucy: Veraunda, tell them what it is like when you have a secret to tell but you are afraid nobody will believe you.

Keisha: What?

Lucy: Tell them what it is like to be a victim of a rape and afraid that nobody will believe you if you tell. Explain the complex range of emotions people experience after being violated physically.

Keisha: THERE IS NO WAY IN HELL WE ARE GOING TO TALK ABOUT BEING RAPED! We can't do it. Writing about it was one thing because you don't have to see their faces as you share your story, but getting up in front of an audience and telling them what happened to you is off limits. We are not going to be able to handle the pressure. It is going to cause you to relive the whole experience every time you tell it. NO WAY, THIS IS A HORRIBLE IDEA!

Lucy: Wait a minute, what if you just submit the proposal and see what happens. If they accept it, then you know you are on the right path. If they say "NO" then we will know it was just a crazy thought on both Mr. Landry's part and my part.

Keisha: Mr. Landry did not suggest sharing OUR story. Mr. Landry suggested using our experience as a sex crimes prosecutor to present to the conference.

Lucy: Veraunda, think very carefully about what I am saying. How many people do you know that are sharing their personal and professional experience to renew the commitment of the men and women working in the sex crimes field? When you attended the weeklong conference for sex crimes professionals you received a lot of technical information. But not once were you moved by the idea that people aren't telling because they fear not being believed.

Keisha: Everybody knows the majority of domestic violence and sex crimes aren't reported because people are afraid. Lucy, you just amaze me! We are too smart for this foolishness you come up with. You are stupid if you think we are going to get up on a stage to share one of the worst experiences we have ever had. It is out of the question!

I was in total agreement with Keisha! I could not do it. I could not *talk* about being raped. I didn't want to talk about being raped! I had tears in my eyes just thinking about it. I had a major struggle writing my story for "Everything Has A Price!" There was no way I could get up in front of strangers and share it.

There will be times on your journey despite your inner struggle, the ideas keep coming. You will not be able to question where they are coming from. The title, "Nobody will believe me!" was powerful. I had a brief description of the session immediately:

When communicating with victims of sex crimes, it is not what you say, but how you say it! As a victim of a rape at the age of sixteen, Veraunda turned that experience into a rewarding career as a prosecutor who advocated for both juvenile and adult victims of sex crimes. This presentation focuses on how to communicate with victims both verbally and nonverbally and how that communication can be used in court.

Before I knew it, I sent the title along with a brief paragraph to the coordinator of the program. A few months later I received a letter stating the committee had chosen my presentation for the 2002 conference in Orlando. I felt a heavy burden about this alleged "opportunity!"

Keisha: Now what are we going to do? Lucy has gotten us into this mess! What are we going to say? What are we going to share with these people for 45 minutes?

Lucy: It will come to you Veraunda, it always does. The deal was simple, if they accepted your presentation, you would know you were on the right path. The door has opened. You need to walk through it and trust the process.

Keisha: Well, how about the small fact this is a FREE engagement. We aren't getting one dime to talk about being raped! This is absurd, it is distressing and I am appalled we have allowed ourselves to be put in this situation!

Lucy: Veraunda, what if you started by reading the story from your book leading the audience to believe you are telling someone else's story. What if you look up at the end and tell them the sixteen year old in the story is you and that nobody believed you?

I got chills just thinking about how powerful the presentation would be. I knew at that moment, Lucy was on to something. I just didn't know how big it would be. I created an outline for the presentation, which mixed my personal story with my professional experience. I said a prayer asking for strength to get through the workshop. In October of 2002 for the first time in my life, I told my story of being raped to a room full of strangers. With tears in my eyes, I read from, "Everything Has A Price!" one detail after another. My hands were trembling and my heart was pounding so hard I swore everybody in the room could hear it. The room was so quiet you could hear my breaths in between sentences. When I reached the end of the story, I put the book down on the table next to me, looked straight into the eyes of my audience and said, "That sixteen year old girl was me!" I heard one lady gasp, and whisper, "Oh my God!" When I looked at her, she was crying with me.

I moved on through the presentation with powerful examples of why people don't tell about being abused. I shared how as men and women in this difficult profession we had to start realizing the important role we played in the healing of a victim who had been violated. I closed with a powerful story of a little girl who had been molested by her mother's boyfriend. When she told a relative and who involved criminal justice system, the mother shipped the little girl off to her native country so she would not testify. As heads shook in disbelief, I closed by saying, "I hope that little girl would not be forever damaged because "her mother did not believe her!"

The response at the conclusion of my presentation was overwhelming! Men and women stood in line to tell me how my hour with them had made a difference. But one woman sent chills through me when she said, "I have been looking for you!" Her name was Joanne, a twenty-five year veteran sex crimes detective who conducted training seminars across the country. She proceeded to tell me my personal and professional experience was something that was in demand. She was in a hurry because she was teaching a session right after mine, but it was no accident she chose to come to my workshop. Her last words were, "I will be in touch soon!"

When I received the email from Joanne inviting me to be the keynote speaker for her international conference I was deeply honored. However, I had no idea that she and a woman by the name of Debbie would create a wealth of opportunities for me to share at conferences around the country. Within a few months I started receiving calls from conferences throughout the nation requesting information on, "Nobody will believe me!" The individuals calling would say, Joanne and Debbie said you kept them on the edge of their seat. I was thankful for the kind words. But I had no clue who Debbie was. I contacted Joanne to track Debbie down. I sent an email thanking her for recommending me to other conferences. Her response was filled with praise about my "Nobody will believe me!" presentation. She felt very strongly about others hearing my message. This was the beginning of a major door opening in an area I had no intention of pursuing.

In July of 2003, I had one of the most inspiring telephone conversations with Mr. Landry. He had outlined an agenda for my career. As he went through the list, I was writing down as much as I could. He made numerous great suggestions but one has made a profound impact on the direction of my career. Kobe Bryant who was a twenty-five-year-old player for the NBA championship Los Angeles Lakers was all over the news because of an alleged rape of a nineteen-year-old resort concierge. Mr. Landry suggested I conduct workshops about sexual misconduct to athletic departments on college campuses. Hmmm, great idea! As a former sex crimes prosecutor I could talk about choices and consequences. Hopefully, I made a positive impact in the decision making process of the athletes. I loved it, I went to work immediately! I created a proposal, then followed up with asking a few key people to write letters of recommendations to be included in my marketing materials. This was the right door at the right time! It swung so fast, I didn't see it coming.

I sent an email requesting recommendations to Joanne, Debbie, Coach Trudi Lacey, the head coach of the WNBA Charlotte Sting and Coach Bill Yoast from the movie, "Remember the Titans!" I was strategically asking people who would create a good balance of Sexual Assault and Athletic Professionals. Everyone responded within a week. I knew I was on the right path. Debbie started sending emails with relevant articles and tremendous words of encouragement for my idea. As I was reading one of the emails from her the voice within said pick up the phone. Just call her!

I dialed the number. When Debbie answered the phone, I asked her if I could share my idea with her. As we proceeded to talk for the first time in our lives, Debbie shared how my presentation had impacted her. There was a shared connection like we had known each other for years. I felt the tears coming because deep down inside I knew this call was no accident. I found myself writing phrases down during our conversation. Lucy was whispering to me:

Lucy: Veraunda, the keynote speaking was door number one leading you into door number two which is the training. Do you realize you could make a tremendous difference in the lives of individuals in the sexual assault and domestic violence profession?

The topics were coming to me quicker than I could write them down. As I developed them into presentations I was sharing them with Debbie who was in Washington, D.C. supporting me every step of the way! In a few hours I had created a series of presentations specifically for the sexual assault and domestic violence profession. I faxed a draft to Debbie the next morning who instantly started sending my proposal to various agencies that sponsored sex crime conferences. The doors were beginning to open! One after the other, opportunities were presenting themselves. I realized the series of "Nos" were setting me up for the right opportunity at the right time. Within one month of the fourth "No" coming from the college, I had two major doors open that would provide a revolving door allowing me the opportunity to make a difference in the lives of others. The "Nos" were starting to make sense! They appeared to be a puzzle similar to what the kids do in school when they connect the dots. One thing had led to another. The Nos were becoming creative windows of opportunity. The college called me back to offer me a position as an adjunct professor. I accepted! A friend who worked for a local municipality suggested I could assist with her increasing workload by becoming a back up prosecutor for the City. I submitted a proposal for the City Attorney to review. After a few meetings, I was awarded the contract! Instead of one "job" being the source of my income, I was now in a position of having several streams of income which would always allow me to keep EHAP as a priority.

Lucy: Do you see how we have benefited from the series of "Nos?" Veraunda, what looked like a maze is actually a beautiful work of art! You just could not see it while it was being created. One line here, one line there, a splash of red over here, a little bit of blue over there. It never makes sense while you are in the process. But, you have done one thing consistently. You have kept your faith that there was a higher being at work on your behalf! Veraunda, God will always honor your faithfulness!

The doors were being closed for two reasons. First, to keep you on the right path. Deep down inside you have always known, you were not going to be allowed to settle back into a job that would rob you and the nations of your full potential. You were not going to be able to limit the possibilities for EHAP. The doors were closing to make sure you did not harm yourself by taking the wrong job for the wrong reason at the wrong time because of the temporary pressures.

The second reason is because your Creator needed to make sure you would be faithful and practice what you teach. Did you notice when you started writing this book with the title being, "You don't have to settle!" That is when all of the pressures to settle began?"

Wow, the question from my inner voice went to the core of me. Looking back, Lucy was absolutely right. My problems didn't really begin until I was ready to move to the next level of my journey. For the first year and a half things had gone relatively smooth. I had new clients, I was speaking and although I was not out of debt, I was consistently able to pay my bills. I didn't feel like I was drowning when I first started stepped out of the boat. The storm began when I had walked a little distance away from the boat. When I panicked, I thought I could fix the situation on my own by swimming to a place of refuge. But I was told "No!"

- No, you will not be in control!
- No, you will not go back to a place of comfort!
- No, you will not abort the mission!

- No, you will not live an ordinary life, when you have been predestined for an extraordinary journey!
- No, YOU WILL NOT SETTLE!

Even as I write this I feel a sense of astonishment, the last year of "Nos" has been a test to see if I would be able to complete this book with a story of victory rather than complacency. Would I be able to trust the process despite the storms? Would I be able to feel the fear and do it anyway as Dr. Jeffers suggests. Would I be able to see the value in the series of "Nos?"

Yes, I would be able to trust the process, because the "Nos!" were pushing me *through* the process. What have your "Nos" been pushing you to? Have you become distraught and discouraged? Do you feel like giving up? Are you standing in the middle of a long hallway with lots of doors? Do you feel the pressure from all sides closing in on you? Are you trying the doors to see which one will open? Are you panicking because when you try to twist the knob, it is locked? When you go to the next-door do you get angry because the person who answers your frantic knocking simply looks at you before slamming the door in your face? Did you hurt your foot when you got so scared you tried to kick the next door in? Do you feel the throbbing in your foot and head because the door didn't budge?

Shhhhhhh, stop, right where you are! Get very still. Just look around you, there is a door that is cracked. You can see the light seeping through what appears to be a very small opening. Shhhhh, don't say a word yet! Just listen there are angels directing your path. Be patient! Your inner voice is whispering, "No, not this one!" "No, not yet!" "No, not this person!" "No, not this job!" "No, not this time!"

When you experience the series of "Nos" be confident you are on the right path. The right opportunity is so close you will miss it if you get scared and you decide to settle.

Let me share one last thing with you. During the series of "Nos" various individuals would speak to me mysteriously. One week before I finished this chapter an older gentleman pulled me aside after hearing me speak about "change." He asked me if I was a Christian woman. I confirmed I was. He spent the next few minutes telling me he saw me speaking to large audiences around the nation. He saw me on television. He told me God was going to do some extraordinary things through my ministry. Tremendous doors were going to open, taking me to tremendous places. He closed with a chilling statement leaving no doubt in my mind I was having a out-of-body experience to explain the "Nos." His final statement to me was, "I see the vision. You have seen it as well. The vision will become a reality."

I knew exactly what he was talking about. As crazy as it might sound, I understood the message loud and clear. "My dreams were about to become a reality." The day before I finished the chapter Mr. Landry sent me this as the closing of his email:

"By the way, when God was telling you "NO" prior to Friday, July 18, He had *already* ordained you to be the keynote speaker at a conference that will receive an *outstanding* media focus and gently push Veraunda into her dynamic spotlight." Mr. Landry was speaking into my future. He had seen the vision for my life as well!

If you just stop, look and listen, voices of your vision are speaking to you in so many different ways. Listen to them! Embrace them! They are supporting you through the process. They are helping you understand what "No" really means.

Your "Nos" are really preparing you for a resounding "Yes!" at the right time, with the right person and for the right reasons! "No" my friend, simply means NEXT! Refuse to stay where you are! Your Creator is directing your steps. Regardless of your situation trust the process. Refuse to stop! Refuse to settle! No my friend simply means next! Your Creator will honor your faith. Habakkuk 1:17 says, "For the vision is yet for an appointed time. But at the end it will speak and it will not lie. Though it tarries, wait for it. Because surely, *it will come to pass!*"

Apply the lessons in this chapter to your life:

What "Nos" have you experienced in the past?

Looking back can you think of a reason for these "Nos?"

Looking forward, will the series of "Nos" help prepare you for the next opportunity?

You Never Know!

Once you make a decision to step out on faith to pursue your dream you will experience an incredible journey in the world of unknowns. I am constantly amazed at the experiences I have and the people who come into my path as a result of pursuing my vision. Many of those people end up being a link in a chain providing you with wisdom. Others will provide encouragement on your journey becoming great cheerleaders during challenging periods.

When you find yourself wondering what is next for you, the answer will show up in the most unexpected places. In February of 2002, I was asked to speak for the National Consortium of Academics and Sports (NCAS). The organization's headquarters are in Orlando, Florida. Each year they hold a major national conference for various professionals in the athletic arena. Many of the attendees are athletic administrators from various colleges around the country. The conference ends with a spectacular banquet honoring individuals who have made a significant contribution in the world of sports. I've really enjoyed the awards banquet through the years because they honor a wide array of individuals from various walks of life. The stories of the honorees are always of perseverance and overcoming obstacles. I have watched great coaches of high school teams, be honored with track star Jackie Joyner Kersee or basketball coach Carolyn Peck. A high school athlete can share the stage with legends like basketball player Julius Irving or golf legend Lee Elder. It is an awesome event.

The connections in your life will be everyday people who appear as you are "working" on your passion. I met Rosalyn Dunlap at a

"Everything Has A Price!" book discussion hosted by one of my sorority sisters in 2000. It was a small gathering of approximately ten women. Rosalyn purchased the book after the discussion. We instantly connected. Within a week we arranged a lunch meeting. I know very little about collegiate or professional sports. On the surface, it appeared Rosalyn and I would have very little in common. Our initial connection was Rosalyn's vision to write a book. Your passion for your vision will connect you to the right people for the right reason at the right time. Rosalyn, would be a connection to a huge blessing.

A week before the 2002 NCAS conference, the committee decided to have a speaker for the final luncheon scheduled for almost two hundred athletic administrators from around the country. Rosalyn was the Associate Director for NCAS but had not been involved in the conference planning prior to this point. However, because of the short notice, the committee approached Rosalyn for a possible speaker from the Central Florida area. Rosalyn's suggestion of me to the committee was a miracle in the making. It was an unusual recommendation because I had no athletic background not to mention not one single athletic bone in my body. You never know how life will open doors when you least expect them. What Rosalyn knew was I would deliver a powerful presentation regardless of who the audience was.

When I received the inquiry from Rosalyn, I was honored. I immediately accepted. I knew my calendar was clear because I have attended the recognition banquet held at Disney's Wide World of Sports every year since I met Rosalyn. This year would be no different. The luncheon was scheduled on the same day as the closing banquet. There was one catch. There was no money in the budget to pay for my speaking. I trusted Rosalyn as a friend enough to know she would not ask me to do something that would not lead to some type of positive exposure. There was an opportunity here. I just didn't know how big the opportunity was until I arrived.

This year's banquet honorees included Coach Bill Yoast and Coach Herman Boone whose life story was portrayed in the Disney movie "Remember the Titans." I, like millions of other people had watched this movie about a white football coach loosing his job to a black football coach during desegregation in Alexandria, Virginia. The movie depicts their lives during a difficult transition period, which leads the team to a stellar season despite color barriers. I thought it was a great movie! The thought of meeting the coaches never crossed my mind. However, I was looking forward to seeing them honored during the banquet later that evening.

It is my practice to arrive early when speaking for an event. I still experience nervous energy prior to speaking. I was particularly nervous for the NCAS event because it was an audience accustomed to hearing sports professionals speak. I was prepared to give a speech entitled, "You Never Know!" which focuses on the ability each one of us has to make a difference in the lives of others. I arrived over thirty minutes early. I set up my books, business cards, and brochures for display on the table provided in the front of the room. Rosalyn had jetted in for a last check to make sure the tables were set properly for the luncheon. A few of the servers were coming in and out, but for the most part I was in this large room with beautiful chandeliers alone. I felt the butterflies in my stomach fluttering as I finished the display. I decided I would review my outline one last time before the audience started to arrive.

About this time, an older white gentleman with gray hair walked in the room. He was tall with a nice slender build, dressed in khaki slacks and a white short sleeve polo shirt. "Well, so much for reviewing my notes!" I thought. I slid the outline back in the black leather binder, then walked over to greet him with a handshake. I extended my right hand while introducing myself, " Hi, I am Veraunda." His response was one filled with delight. "Oh, you are the woman I was coming to see!" Then he introduced himself, "Hi, I am Bill Yoast." Oh, my Lord! I really felt the butterflies in my stomach now. I am not a person who is star struck. I have met people from all walks of life over the years. However, I was standing in a room all alone with the man who was being honored tonight because of his ability to make a difference by coaching a high school football team. A movie had been inspired to honor his life and dedication to others. Why was he coming to hear me speak??? What could I share that he didn't already know? Part of my brain was thinking about how cool this moment was. The other part of my brain was freaking out because this was a once in a lifetime experience!

Coach Yoast has a very warm presence. He reminds me of a gentle loving grandfather. He is very approachable. His words are soft spoken accompanied by a sincere smile. In fact, if I had to describe him in one word, I would immediately say humble. Coach Yoast told me his family had joined him on the trip to support him as he received the award with Coach Boone. His children and grandchildren wanted to enjoy the Disney theme parks. Coach Boone would not arrive until late in the afternoon. Coach Yoast had agreed to speak for an afternoon session. Instead of playing in the theme parks he was going to take part in some of the conference activities. While browsing through the conference program, he read my bio then decided he should come hear me speak. I was flattered to say the least!

After he told me why he was here, I started sharing with Coach Yoast what a privilege it was to meet him. I told him I was inspired by his journey with Coach Boone. I was also touched by the courage it must have taken to make some of the decisions during a racially charged period in our country. I have always been thankful for the sacrifices of the men and women of all races during the Civil Rights movement. I am very clear I stand on the shoulders of those individuals who stood in the face of adversity to pave the way for people like me to live my dream regardless of my gender or race. Coach Yoast and Coach Boone were just two of those individuals. Their lives, like all of ours is a constant roller coaster ride full of ups and downs. When Coach Boone, an African American, received the head coach position, it was an example of life throwing Coach Yoast an unknown card to see what he was going to do with it. Coach Yoast and Coach Boone had no idea that doing the difficult thing for the right reasons would produce such tremendous rewards. Though their story wasn't made into a movie until 2000, they had been changing lives for over thirty years without any need for recognition or praise.

Coach Yoast was gracious as I sung his praises, "Veraunda, all we did was coach a high school football team. Now, tell me about you." I responded by telling him I didn't know what to say. The short story was I was a former prosecutor who wrote a book entitled, *Everything Has a Price!* Now, I was traveling the country trying to empower and inspire others to live their dreams. By this time, Rosalyn had returned to greet the athletic administrators as they entered the room. Our conversation was cut short as we were directed to our seats. Coach Yoast was seated next to me at the front table. As the program started, he leaned over to whisper he wanted to purchase my book at the end of the luncheon. I felt my nerves fluttering again. I said a quiet prayer asking for my words to make a difference in the lives of each person in the audience.

After the introduction, I stood up with my legs shaking. Normally to break the ice in the room I start by asking a question. Today was no different. I asked the audience to turn to their neighbor then ask a simple question, "Why are *you* here?" There was laughter during the exchange of reasons among the audience. Once it settled, I told the audience:

Every single day, you have the opportunity to make a difference in the lives of others, the key is you never know how you will impact someone's life or how they will impact yours. Every day, ordinary people make extraordinary differences in the lives of others by believing in their dreams and developing their potential. My message to you today is simply, You Really Never Know!

I continued by sharing the story of my seventh grade English teacher Mrs. Miller who looked beyond my attitude to see my talent as a speaker. Her dedication to making sure I used my mouth in a productive manner was the reason I became an orator, a radio personality, a television host, an attorney, and a national speaker. Mrs. Miller taught for over thirty years. She came to work every day with the belief that she could make a difference.

Toward the end of my presentation, I included Coach Yoast and Coach Boone's story. Who would have thought two men who grew up in poverty in segregated neighborhoods, would be thrown together based on their love of coaching high school football? Who knew that Coach Yoast making a decision to stay with Coach Boone as an assistant coach would change his life forever? See you never know!

Who knew the football players of T.C. Williams high school would still be making a difference over thirty years later based on their love of football. Desegregation forced them to learn how to work together as a team if they wanted to continue to play football. Who knew the Titans would be an example of how diversity can be successful for generations to come? No one knew! The coaches, the players, the parents and the students of T.C. Williams high school pushed through the challenges to become an example to athletic programs, corporate offices and governmental agencies around the country. I closed the speech by reminding my audience their jobs were not about athletics, they were about using their love of athletics to make a difference in the lives of the students they came in contact with everyday. My final words were:

So I ask you again: Why are YOU here? Remember, every day you have the opportunity to make a difference in someone's life, you never know how you will impact their life or how they will in turn impact yours! God bless each of you as you continue to make a difference!

Coach Yoast started a standing ovation! As I approached my seat, he gave me a warm hug while telling me I had touched him with my words. It is amazing how life offers rewards when you are doing what you are passionate about. You began to attract supporters who become lifelong mentors and friends with very little effort. Coach Yoast was scheduled to speak at two o'clock for a crowd of almost three hundred across the hall. His family would be joining him for his speech. He invited me to stay. He wanted to introduce me to his children. It was my pleasure to meet his daughters, ex-wife, sons-in-law and grandchildren. They were all absolutely delightful. As we chatted, I felt right at home. It seemed as if we were old friends being reunited after years apart. As we moved into the conference hall, Coach Yoast asked me to sit with his family near the front of the room. I responded I'd be there in a minute, I needed to leave my briefcase and promotional materials in the back of the room.

While I was securing the briefcase, the Executive Director and Founder of NCAS, Dr. Richard Lapchick walked up to me with another gentleman who appeared to be in his sixties. Dr. Lapchick shook my hand while expressing his gratitude for my presentation. I expressed my gratitude for this opportunity to make a difference. Dr. Lapchick introduced the man standing next to him. Apparently, while they were in the restroom, the gentleman approached Dr. Lapchick to inquire where they found me. From there the gentleman took over. "I owe you an apology!" I wondered why an apology was needed. I did not have any prior interaction with this gentleman. I had no clue who he was. I was a bit baffled. He went on to say, "When you started the presentation with the question why are you here?, I immediately turned to my neighbor and said, I don't want to hear this philosophical BS." I felt my eyebrows rise in surprise.

I gave a polite smile while asking the gentleman if he really said those words. He responded, "Yes, I sure did! I have been to conference after conference for over forty years as an athletic administrator. You get tired of hearing the same old stuff over and over again. When I saw you, I immediately thought what can this young attorney tell me about why I am here." I wasn't sure how to respond or where this was leading so I continued to listen. He continued, "I have to tell you as you shared your story I was touched. You reminded me how important my job is. Actually, I had been thinking about retiring, but I am rejuvenated now. You made me think about all of the students who have told me I made a difference. You are absolutely right Miss Jackson, you never know!" I was thankful he had shared how my words had made a difference. See you never know how you will impact someone's life or how they, in turn will impact yours. I was living in an awesome moment.

The room was packed by now. There was standing room only as the athletic administrators were joined by employees of the Disney's Wide World of Sports to hear Coach Yoast speak. I hurried to my seat. Coach Yoast brought tears to my eyes when he opened by telling the audience I had reminded him how important it was to seize the opportunity to make a difference. He went on to share his story but incorporated my words numerous times during his speech. Each time he would start the sentence by saying, "As Veraunda said," I was moved by his including my message into his life story. He told the audience he and Coach Boone were doing their best to work through a very difficult set of circumstances. With humility he said, "All we did was coach a high school football team." As he closed he said, "As Veraunda just reminded me, you never know what's going to happen." He never dreamed a movie would be made. He never dreamed of speaking around the country for conferences, colleges and major corporations.

Almost thirty years later, a young man visiting the town was in the barbershop when he heard some guys talking of a reunion for the

Titans. He asked who the Titans were. Once he heard the story, he met with Coach Yoast and Coach Boone to ask permission to write a screenplay. The screenplay was bought by Disney. The movie has created awesome opportunities for the coaches and players. You never know!

I certainly never thought speaking for NCAS would have provided the opportunity for me to meet Coach Yoast. I certainly had no idea my words would have such an affect that he would end up quoting me in his presentation. However, here I was sitting in a room with three hundred other people who were enjoying the opportunity! But it doesn't stop there. After Coach Yoast finished speaking he signaled for me not to leave after he spoke. I obliged. He asked me to join them at their family table for the banquet. I wasn't sure this could be arranged because there was assigned seating done ahead of time.

Imagine my delight when I arrived for the dinner and one of the greeters seated me with Coach Yoast's family near the front of a six-hundred seat banquet room. Coach Yoast immediately came over to greet me with a hug. He said he had a gift for me. He handed me an autographed photo. The picture included Coach Yoast, Coach Boone with actors Denzel Washington and Will Patton. I was elated!

The night was wonderful! As I watched each honoree receive their awards I could not help thinking about how each of them had followed their love for athletics with unlimited possibilities waiting for them. Life was rewarding them for working harder, dreaming bigger and refusing to settle! The choices Coach Yoast and Coach Boone along with the players and parents had to make as a football team being integrated were agonizing as portrayed in the movie. Every area of their lives was affected by a decision to continue with the team. The bottom line for the coaches was despite the obstacles, they loved their jobs, they loved the game of football, not to mention they had tremendous desire to win! They used the concept of teamwork to create national champions!

No matter what situation you are in, you must remember the positive possibilities are endless. Life rewards people who refuse to settle. Many times those rewards are in ways you would never imagine.

Coach Yoast and I have remained friends since 2002. In 2003, he was traveling to St. Petersburg, Florida with his family to support his daughter in an athletic competition on the beach. I was invited to spend the day with them. I made the hour and half drive on a beautiful Saturday morning in August.

You never know what will happen on any given day when you start living your dreams. It just so happened actor Will Patton was shooting a movie in Tampa. Mr. Patton did a great job of portraying Coach Yoast in the movie "Remember the Titans." Mr. Patton joined us for a glorious day on the beach. We had a delightful breakfast together. After the breakfast, we were joined by one of the original 1971 Titans who now lives in St. Petersburg. He met us to watch the competition. We moved to the beach to cheer for Coach Yoast's daughter Deedee as she competed. The sun was shining, the breeze was blowing. I felt my spirit rejoicing because I was witnessing how our Creator orchestrates daily miracles.

After the competition was over, everyone kind of scattered. Coach Yoast's kids were going to grab lunch. The grandkids wanted to swim in the hotel pool. I wanted to enjoy the breeze coming from the ocean. I found a lounge chair near some palm trees in a shaded area. I arranged the chair so I was facing the beach. I kicked my feet up, exhaled, then started reading a magazine. Quietly, I was saying a prayer of thanks. Thanks for this opportunity. Thanks for the confirmation I was on the right track. Thanks for the daily reminder that you never know!

About thirty minutes later, Coach Yoast pulled up a chair next to me. We talked about my mother passing the year before, the movie, his family and this book. Will Patton joined us in the shade after a swim in the ocean. I never imagined life would bring me to conversations on the beach with legendary sports figures or well-known actors. There was a common theme as we chatted throughout the day. Each of us were very ordinary people, who started with a desire to do something we loved. Each of us had to find our inner strength to survive. Each of us had to dig deep to hold onto our faith while enduring the constant challenges as we pursued our passion. Each of us had been on the roller coaster of barely making enough money, friends disappointing us, family tragedy and learning from our mistakes. I learned so much from these two men about infinite possibilities. I learned you never know how "great" people really are until you have the opportunity to spend quality time with them. I learned everyone started somewhere. I was reminded every journey begins with a step. As we shared our various stories, Coach Yoast and Mr. Patton confirmed, *Everything Has A Price!* But if you refuse to settle, your vision will become a reality!

The longer I pursue this passion of speaking, the more I am convinced you have to be open to the possibilities of every individual. Each person you meet has the potential of being a connector. People will come and go as you progress through various stages of your vision. Things are not always as they appear and neither are people. However, everything happens for a reason! Remember there are no accidents in this life. If things don't work out the way you planned them, have no fear! Things are still working in your favor even if you don't see it or understand it at the time. Everything will work out for your good. You never know what lies behind an unsuccessful attempt.

While working with my athletic clients, there was discussion about finding a way to empower professional female athletes. Immediately, I embraced their vision! There was one problem. I didn't know very many professional women who were also athletes. Ok, I'll be totally honest, I had no connections in the sports world! After much discussion, we decided my company would coordinate the event. The athletes would provide the names of outstanding women who were well respected within the industry. I was responsible for contacting the women to explain the program then inviting them to participate as speakers. I began calling complete strangers, asking them to join us in making a difference in the lives of female athletes. The prospective speakers were responding with a lot of enthusiasm. I was becoming very excited as I made the calls. The women told me they thought it was a great idea and pledged their support.

One of my final calls was to the WNBA Charlotte Sting organization. Felicia Hall was the director of business operations for the Sting. Prior to joining the Sting, she was the manager of the NIKE Women's Basketball Sports Marketing Division. Her ability to reach our athletes would be tremendous because of her dynamic story. Felicia was a three-year letter winner at the University of Iowa, where she played under Hall of Fame Coach Vivian Stringer. After graduating with a bachelor's degree in elementary education and teaching the fifth grade, she attended the University of Iowa's Law School, earning her Juris Doctorate in 1995. She was a great example of how young ladies can use athletics combined with academics to pursue their passion.

With all of this information, I picked up the phone praying she would say yes to our invitation. I started by telling her I was a former prosecuting attorney who changed careers. I also explained the program and why we wanted her to join us as a speaker. Towards the end of the conversation, Felicia asked me, "What did you say you did again?" I explained I was a full-time professional speaker, consultant and speech coach. I could hear the enthusiasm in her voice as she said she was interested in a career as a motivational speaker. The more we talked, the clearer it was this phone call was not a coincidence. I was scheduled to visit Durham, North Carolina a few weeks later so we set up a meeting in Charlotte. You never know how one person will connect you to another person. I have started to realize this life is full of linking. One person links you to another person, which keeps you moving in the right direction.

When I arrived in Charlotte, North Carolina, Felicia picked me up from the train station. She had arranged for us to attend a holiday luncheon prior to our meeting to discuss the speaking industry. We stopped by her office to pick up Trudi Lacey. Coach Lacey was the Assistant Coach of the Sting. Felicia asked me if I minded Coach Lacey joining us for the meeting after lunch. I absolutely did not mind her joining us. After all, you never know how you are going to bless someone, or how they in turn will bless you.

Coach Trudi as I affectionately call her now, is a legend in her own right, but you would never know it if you waited on her to tell you. At almost six feet tall with a slender build, her appearance has athlete written all over it. She was very soft-spoken, yet very approachable. You never know to whom you are talking. I am always amazed by people who stick their nose up in the air at other people. I make it my business to speak to everyone, including housekeepers in the halls of hotels, custodians in airports, secretaries in offices, receptionists on the phone. Everybody starts somewhere. Just as I started out at McDonald's as a teenager, then I drove a bus to pay my way through college and temped to make ends meet while writing this book. *Everybody* is trying to work their way through their present situations. None of us is any better than anyone else! We are all on this journey called life, so how we treat each other becomes vital to our individual success.

I repeat, you never know who you are talking to. You never know what their future holds. Often people who think they have "arrived" dismiss or ignore people they perceive as "not on the same level." You should never be jealous of someone else's good fortune. You should never wish someone ill will. There is a universal law, what goes around will come back around. Be careful how you treat people while trying to achieve your success. The people you step on climbing up the ladder of success, will be the same people you will pass on the way down when some one else kicks you in the head trying to climb over you.

On the other hand, if you have been a person of integrity who acknowledged everyone along your journey, those people will remember your kindness, your hard work and your professionalism. People will support you if you have acknowledged their worth as you have interacted with them. How you treat people in the present determines how you will be treated in the future!

I had no idea who Coach Trudi *really* was. I didn't know a whole lot about the female sports industry. However, I believed if there was a way I could help encourage her in the speaking industry, there was no reason for me not to. When you give freely, you will always receive a blessing. As I have grown in this profession as a speaker and as an author, there have been numerous people who helped me without expecting anything in return. They simply believed in my vision. I adopted this practice very early on when I started EHAP. I may not be able to help everyone, but I will return calls and I will respond to emails. When I find I can't help someone, I will try to provide alternatives to help them pursue their vision. When there is an opportunity to give back, I am going to seize it. My meeting with Felicia and Coach Trudi was an opportunity to share what I had learned from my first two years in the industry with two women who wanted to pursue their passion of speaking. You simply never know what will happen down the road! I was making an investment in them, just as others had invested in me.

Coach Trudi joined the Sting as the Assistant Coach during the 2001 season which was one of the greatest turnarounds in professional sports history. She had worked with USA Basketball in addition to the Gold Medal 2000 Women's Olympic Basketball Team. Coach Trudi was the head coach for the University of South Florida for eight years before joining the WNBA. She was an All-American who was honored by her alma mater, North Carolina State University when they retired her jersey in 2000. She earned her undergraduate degree in business followed by her masters in education administration. She had also founded Life Coach Designs, a personal and business consulting company which specialized in helping individuals, athletic teams and corporations excel both personally and professionally. I did not know any of this when we met.

Coach Trudi listened intently as I gave a whirlwind consultation about getting started in the speaking industry. I was trying to squeeze in as much as I could during our meeting. We ran through organization, scheduling, contracts and marketing. Three hours flew by before I knew it. It was time for me to head back to Durham. My train would be leaving soon. As I left, I told Coach Trudi what a pleasure it was to have met her. I also let her know if there was anything I could do for her I was only a phone call or email away. Little did I know Coach Trudi would turn out to be a great friend and supporter.

I have always admired one of my friends for her spirit of discernment. Her name is Monica and she is very good at seeing people for who they really are. I can remember entering into a business venture that Monica immediately and accurately forecasted would not work because the other person lacked personal integrity. I began to pray for wisdom and discernment in my daily interactions with people. Slowly, I started to learn when I meet people I should try to feel their spirit, see their vision and let their actions speak louder than their words. Many people talk a good game. They make promises they have no intentions of keeping. They say what they think you want to hear. When you follow up with a phone call, email or letter, they fail to respond. I have started to pay attention to these actions. They speak volumes about your value to these people! There is a scripture I love, "Do not despise the days of small beginnings!" (Zechariah 4:10) In other words, you never know where you or anyone else that you connect with will end up on this journey!

Coach Trudi had a humble spirit. She instantly sent me a thank you card for the time I had spent sharing with her, along with a check for a copy of my book, *"Everything Has A Price!"* Many people I meet expect a free copy of my book. Coach Trudi had declined this offer indicating she knew I was a business woman who had bills to pay. I was impressed with her professionalism not to mention her investing in my work as a writer. She had a sharing spirit. When I told her I liked her personalized thank you card, she told me how she did it, then encouraged me to create one for EHAP.

Coach Trudi had an awesome vision. She wanted to become the head coach of a WNBA team in addition to developing a successful speaking career. Her actions spoke louder than her words. She was a person who followed through. When I mentioned how non-athletic I was, she volunteered to help me come up with a plan to eat better while exercising on a more consistent basis. Coach Trudi became my personal trainer helping me shed fifteen pounds by checking in on me weekly. Despite her hectic recruiting schedule, we would talk via cell phones at least once a week. She showed a genuine interest in my vision, my success, and my personal well-being. Our consistent communication was forming a foundation for what is now a blossoming friendship.

You never know how life will reward you on this journey. I am constantly reminded people are a part of the ultimate way our Creator blesses us here on earth. When I met Coach Trudi, I did not have a list of her credentials. I did not have to know who she was to help her. When you are on the right path, you don't have to know everything or everybody. All you have to do is have a sincere interest in blessing others. Sure, there will be people who take advantage of your kindness or talent. Those are the people who have forgotten what you sow is what you reap. Don't waste your time fretting over what you gave to them. When you invest in the lives of others you can never live in lack. Your focus has to remain on giving from your heart, not with an expectation of receiving it back. Remember you never know how life will repay your acts of kindness.

Despite having totally different professional backgrounds, our desire to make a difference through our speaking brought us together. When you are on the right path, you will be connected with people with like spirits who will gladly travel with you or cheer for you when you need support. Coach Trudi and I started discussing ways we could combine our messages to help empower others. We designed an empowerment seminar for women entitled, "The ball is in your court!" This was the first of several projects we collaborated on. Our delivery styles are very different. Coach Trudi is soft-spoken yet very powerful. I am very candid yet practical. We are dynamic together. Our very different personalities make us very effective as a team.

In 2003, Coach Trudi was named the head coach for the Charlotte Sting. Her vision to be a head coach in the WNBA became a reality! Who would have thought a prosecuting attorney would become a friend with a professional women's basketball coach, then team up to empower others? See you never know!

Remember, I had partnered with a colleague to start a female sports agency? I enjoyed the thought of working with athletes, but not recruiting or trying to secure clients. For a short period of time, I lost my focus. I was headed in the right direction, but wasn't clear what my role would be with the sports industry. Because I was unclear, I was willing to try what seemed like a great idea at the time. When that partnership did not work out, I quickly decided I wanted out of the sports world. What else would I be able to do with athletes? However, the first athlete who approached me was very interested in speaking professionally. That young lady hired me as her speech coach. As I began speech coaching and writing for her, I realized the possibilities were endless. I had to remain open to them. One athlete client led to another athlete client, which led to a great idea, which led to my meeting Coach Trudi.

I would work with professional athletes! But not in the way I had previously thought. Sometimes what appears to be a complete disaster is really a period of transition. When the winds of life seem to be destroying everything around you, remember the things that are deeply rooted shall not be moved. When all is said and done, the people who are of true spirit will remain with you. The people who are blown away by small amounts of wind were never meant to endure the journey. They were simply connectors.

I am so thankful for my original partnership leading to the sports agency. I would have never imagined myself working in the sports industry had it not been for my partner's idea to start a female sports agency. I am so thankful the partnership connected me with a WNBA player who inquired about my services as a speech coach. I am so thankful the player became a client who shared an incredible amount of time teaching me about the sports industry, especially basketball. I am thankful that an idea to help other female athletes led me to Felicia who unselfishly invited Coach Trudi to join us to talk about professional speaking. Do you see how my passion, my love of speaking continues to bring me full circle? You never know where your passion will take you.

In 2003, Coach Trudi hired me to conduct a public speaking workshop for her team. This workshop provided me with the honor of meeting one of the greatest point guards in the WNBA. For two years, I had been talking about Dawn Staley, an Olympic gold medalist who was also the head coach of the women's basketball at Temple University. I had consistently read about her work in the community. Her spirit of giving was incredible. She was so well respected in her hometown of Philadelphia that they painted a seven-story portrait in her honor on a building. I knew my workshop had to exceed the players' expectations, but I found myself wondering, is Dawn Staley as real as everyone thinks she is? I decided to find out.

Throughout the lunch break prior to my workshop, I spoke to players on the team to see how they would treat an unknown visitor. I was pleasantly surprised when every single player greeted me despite being hungry and tired. When I spoke to Dawn, I went one step further. After our initial exchange of hellos, I told her she had a homework assignment. She looked a bit surprised, but stayed very cordial. I explained I would be conducting the professional development workshop later that afternoon. I wanted her to come up with three main reasons why community service was important. Dawn smiled while replying, "I'll be ready."

During my workshop, I told the young ladies, you never know who you are talking to or what impact you have on their lives. I explained it was vital for them to realize each time they spoke in public or attended a public event they had an opportunity to make a difference in the lives of others. I proceeded to tell the players what an impact Dawn Staley's community service had on me over the past five years as I watched the WNBA games. I shared with them how Dawn had inspired me, a person with no athletic talent or knowledge, to create a program for high school female athletes.

When the professional empowerment seminar that originally connected me with Felicia and Coach Trudi was canceled by my clients, I was livid! How dare this project be canceled after all of the hard work by me and the volunteer committee! With a heavy spirit I visited the WNBA Website to update our mailing list. I was preparing to send letters of regret informing the players in the league of the cancellation. On the home page was an article about Dawn spending some time with some teenage girls during the off-season. The light went off in my head! Start younger! Stay focused! Don't abandon the vision! Re-energize, refocus, then redevelop the program for high school female athletes.

The planning committee and I unanimously agreed to refocus our energy to empower young female athletes to combine their love of sports with a solid education. Our program was a resounding success! You never know how life is going to connect you. Despite the obstacles, seize the opportunities in each situation. It took us a year to redesign the program. However, we had an all-star cast including:

- Dr. Richard Lapchick, Executive Director of NCAS as our opening speaker.
- Television sports commentator Debbie Antonelli.
- Coach Julie Garner who helped start Nike's women's golf program and was the Women's Golf Coach of the Year for SCC and the NCAA division II conferences in 2003.
- Charlotte Campbell who is a US Amateur golf champion attending Rollins College in Orlando.
- Rosalyn Dunlap who held the world record for the Track and Field 600 meters.
- Our closing speaker was none other than Felicia Hall who had started her own company, Felicia Hall and Associates! Her vision had become a reality.

Oh, did I forget to mention we had the honor of Ericka Dunlap joining us to sing "America." Speaking of you never know, Ericka was a former member of the NAACP Youth Council when I was the advisor in the mid 1990's. Ericka was a teenager when I met her. I had no idea what her future held, however, I knew Ericka was extremely talented with a beautiful spirit. Her outer beauty only mirrored how she interacted with me every time I asked her to come speak for a youth event. She gladly accepted my invitations over the years proudly wearing her crowns while encouraging young people to live their dreams. In April of 2003, when she joined me for the sports empowerment seminar she held the title of Miss City Beautiful representing Orlando, Florida. Imagine my pride a few months later when she became the first African American crowned Miss Florida. As of the printing of this book, Ericka is enjoying her reign as Miss America! See you never know! There are infinite possibilities for every single one of us as long as we refuse to settle!

Coach Trudi was unable to join us for the first annual "Off the Court!" because of a conflicting WNBA commitment; however, she gave me her full support including autographing fifty pictures as gifts for our student athletes. Four years after the initial introduction of a possibility to work with athletes by creating an empowerment seminar, EHAP Inc. hosted its first female athlete event in April of 2003. In May of 2003, I was closing my first professional development workshop for the WNBA Charlotte Sting by hugging Dawn Staley and thanking her for making a difference in my life. Incredible!!! You really never know!

Oh, and as a preview, our 2004 keynote speakers include Coach Bill Yoast and Coach Herman Boone. Yep, from the movie "Remember the Titans!" I would have never imagined my company would be hosting events with such incredible people joining in supporting my vision to make a difference. That is what I mean when I say there are infinite possibilities when you take a step of faith to pursue your passion and embrace the vision. You never ever know what door will open for you next. This chapter has come full circle, because my opening statement was:

Once you make a decision to step out on faith to pursue your dream you will experience an incredible journey in the world of unknowns. I have been constantly amazed at the experiences I have and the people who come into my path as I am living my dream. Many of those people end up being a link in a chain that will provide you with wisdom while encouraging you on your journey. When you find yourself wondering what is next for you, the answer will show up in the most unexpected places with some of the most unexpected people.

I'll close this chapter with one last you never know:

When I decided I was going to take the leap into the world of motivational speaking, I didn't know any other professional speakers. I was in the hair salon when another patron asked if I had ever heard of Jewel Diamond Taylor. I had not. She gave me her website. I visited the website and followed up with an email. Jewel responded almost immediately. She was a great source of inspiration.

But it wasn't until I *saw* my dream being lived that the vastness of it hit me. I received a copy of "The Crisis," a magazine published by the NAACP in November of 1999. Inside was a feature story on a motivational speaker by the name of Les Brown. What caught my eye was the photo. Les was sitting on a fountain outside of his Michigan Mansion. It was a tranquil setting. Not only was he at home in the photo, he was clearly at peace.

When I began to read the article, my heart started beating fast. Les Brown was an international speaker with an amazing story. He grew up in poverty, didn't have a college degree and was adopted by Ms. Mammie Brown. Despite others glim forecast for his future, Les made it and made it big! He was a Michigan Senator, a radio personality, and the host of the nationally syndicated Les Brown Show. When I read he had made millions from speaking I said a quiet prayer. I was seeing my dream and what it looked like in "real life!"

I continued to read and my heart leaped for joy when I saw Les used his wealth to help others in various ways. I said another prayer, "Lord, I don't want to be wealthy for me. I want to be able to bless others." When I finished the article, I was so inspired! I wasn't *thinking I could do it! I KNEW I could do it!* I cut the article out of the magazine and put it on the top of my encouragement file. I also started a "blessing diary." The essence of the diary is as I see causes and situations that I want to donate to, I write them down. When the wealth comes I will be able to go down the list and give accordingly.

Three years after reading the article, I received a call from a colleague on a Saturday afternoon. She asked me if I was in town.

Yes, I was, but I was very tired from teaching at the Law Enforcement Academy all day. The next question reminded me, "You never know what's in store for you!" "Veraunda, would you like to have dinner with Les Brown?" I wanted to scream, girl stop playing! Instead, I remained calm and said you mean would I like to go to a dinner where Les Brown is speaking? She said, "No, actually have dinner with Les." My heart was beating fast just like when I read the article. I was receiving the opportunity to meet the inspiration for my dream. Wow! Yes! I would love to have dinner with Les! She told me she would give my number to the contact. They would call me back. Within five minutes the phone rang. It wasn't his people, it was him! Les Brown was talking with me like we were old friends! We made the arrangements for dinner but before we hung up, Les asked me to bring him a copy of my book and any tapes I had. I was excited! I didn't know what would come of our meeting, but holding on to the theory, "You never know!" I packaged the tapes, book and presentation folder to take with me.

When I met Les, he gave me a warm embrace. I watched him as we moved through various settings. People recognized him instantly. He was humble and gracious each time someone sung his praises. He was sincere in his comments to them. His presence was powerful! I was taking it all in.

When we finally sat down for dinner I listened intensely to his words of wisdom for the individuals who dropped in at the table just to have a minute with the famous speaker. The questions ranged from how do you choose topics to how do you get people to book you. But I had a very different area of interest. I wanted to know what was the hardest part of living his dream. As the author of a book telling people that "Everything Has A Price!" I wanted to know about what he had paid to be where he is. I wanted to know about the work behind the glamour.

Les shared some profound wisdom with me that evening. The time passed quickly, before I knew it four hours had passed. As I said good night to Les, he said I would be hearing from him. I told him he did not give me a card, so I had no way to reach him. He said I didn't need a card, he would definitely be in touch. Now, the skeptic in me said, he is being polite and I get the hint, don't call me, I'll call you.

Imagine my surprise when two days later, Les called to say he had listened to my tape and loved it! Les and I continued to speak on a regular basis after our initial meeting. In one conversation he said, "We will be sharing platforms." I held onto that forecast. A few months later, I received a call from United States Congresswoman Corrine Brown's office asking me if I would moderate an event where Les was going to be the keynote speaker. I accepted and had a chance to tell this story during my introduction of Les. You really never know!

Apply the lesson in this chapter to your life:

Have you ever been in a situation where your perseverance provided the opportunity to connect with special individuals who have aided you on your journey.

List those individuals and describe how they ended up being a link in the chain that provided you with wisdom or encouragement on your journey:

When are you going to be on Oprah?

As I travel the country I am constantly asked when I am going to be on Oprah? Sometimes, people tell me they have seen me on Oprah. Other people have told me they have sent an email to Oprah about the book or me. And of course, people are always encouraging me to write Oprah or send her my materials. I have found this to be an interesting journey. I have had a theory since I wrote my first book: People will tell you what they want, what they need and most importantly what they see in you!

This can be a two-way street. You have to be careful not to let other people create a negative journey for you. When people ask me about Oprah or tell me I'm the next Oprah, I take it as the ultimate compliment and a reminder of what is possible. I am humbled by other people seeing my talent and wanting me to excel. In the same breath, I feel some pressure. I wonder if I should be reaching for Oprah's level of success or trust my own vision to take me to places I can't even conceive. Be careful that you don't let others ideas of your success cause you to question your destiny or strive for a place you may not be destined to go.

I can remember hearing one of my favorite speakers, Joyce Meyers, talk about how she prayed and prayed to be on television. Specifically, she wanted a talk show. The talk show became a reality. However, she honestly admits she talked more than the guests did. She also admits being a talk show host was not her calling in life. Instead, she is a great teacher to the masses. If you have ever seen her ministry on Christian television she speaks to thousands and thousands in Convention Centers around the world. It's really awesome! I have never seen her on the Oprah Winfrey Show, yet she is just as successful and making a tremendous impact on millions of lives around the world.

Not many people know this, but I have been on Oprah. It was one of the coolest things I have ever done in my life. When I was in law school I visited a friend in Chicago. When she asked me what I wanted to do in Chicago, I immediately said let's try to get tickets for the Oprah Winfrey Show! I was sitting on the end of one of the front rows. Imagine my delight when Oprah came over during a commercial break, sat down on the steps next to me and started talking to me! The show was about mother-daughter relationships. During the break we chatted about the double-edged practices in parent-child relationships. When the commercials ended she came back to me and said, "You were saying?" I was on national television! I thought I had arrived! The same week I was also on the Jenny Jones show. (This was when she was still doing real people shows and addressing real issues.) For weeks after the shows aired I was a superstar in college. It has been many years since those shows were on. I am sure no one remembers them now. It is a reality check; there is only value in what you are doing today!

When I work with athletes and entertainers they constantly tell me you are only as good as your last win or chart topper. You can score the winning point on Monday and have a wonderful interview after the game with the reporters praising you for your performance. On Wednesday, you lose the game by missing the final shot and the same commentator who was praising you on Monday will trash you and question your abilities. We humans are much like pendulums. We swing back and forth. Very seldom are we with you all the way. When you say something we don't like, we criticize. When you do something to disappoint us, we struggle with forgiveness. When you wear clothes we don't like, we gossip. So there is much wisdom in not depending on people for the ultimate fulfillment. You have to find a balance in your life. You have to be focused. Most importantly, you have to be determined to make it against all odds!

In my first book I said, "People or circumstances will make you feel like you are on top of the world, but what they don't tell you is that those people or circumstances end up controlling your world." My point is simply, I can't let anyone or anything be the ultimate goal for me. When I set goals like, I won't "arrive" until I am Oprah, I am limiting myself! I am settling. I am subconsciously saying I can only go so far without Oprah. I am also devaluing the importance of what I am doing today. I can't afford to limit myself or put myself in a box because there are too many possibilities within my reach everyday. One of my favorite things to tell a crowd is everyday we have the opportunity to make a difference in the lives of someone else. We can get caught up in other people's vision for us and miss our opportunity to touch a life.

Allowing others to determine your worth or position is dangerous. I've tried this many times since starting my own company. On one occasion I worked for an entity that tried to fit me into a *position* instead of using my talents where they worked best. It was a constant struggle. I wanted to work there. I wanted to make a positive contribution not to mention the pay was good. But all the good intentions on both my side and my employers' side didn't work. Why? I wasn't where I was supposed to be. I was trying to do what other people thought was best for me. I was miserable. There were constant questions about what I was doing and why. On the other hand, I have NEVER had to struggle when I was speaking. Why? It is what I was made to do! I am comfortable on stages and behind microphones. It is the one time I am completely free without any questions! It's the one place I am totally confident. It is the one place that others constantly affirm my desire and my ability to make a difference. There are a few skeptics, some critics, but overall, they don't phase me because I know speaking is my gift.

I admire Oprah tremendously. I really admire how she has continuously traveled to new frontiers. When things become constant, she becomes creative. When she was sued by the cattle industry for making a statement, she broadcast her talk show daily from Texas. It would have been easier for Oprah to pay some large amount of money to her accusers or offer a public apology to the beef industry to settle the case. She knew the allegations against her were false, she believed in herself and her right to freedom of speech. Instead of going into a deep depression or hiding because adversity had hit her camp, she looked at the possibilities, then kept doing what she does best. She kept working on her shows to make a positive difference. During one of the most difficult and public trials in her life she kept broadcasting! Oprah didn't stop, nor did she settle!

When I first published the book, "Everything Has A Price!" I sent a copy to Oprah. I'd be crazy not to try to get selected as one of her guests or book club selections. I have read everything published on Oprah. I love her! I love what she has been able to do with her gift of communication. She is indeed an incredible example of what can happen when you pursue your passion. But I believe the most significant thing about Oprah is how she reminds me that my own vision is more than possible!

I am quite clear I don't have to follow in Oprah's footsteps. I am on my own journey. I can honor her for being who she is without trying to be her! So many of us want to do what other people are doing. Stop and just be yourself. Just like our Creator made Oprah, He made you and me. There are millions of successful people who don't have talk shows, or speak for a living. Each one of us has a divine purpose waiting on us to wake up and start living our dreams one day at a time. It's not about being the next Oprah; it's about being the best you!

Of course, I would love to be on Oprah. I believe our paths will connect again. So the question becomes what do I do in the meantime? If am only focusing on getting on her show, what does that say about who I really am? My mission for EHAP is to make a difference in lives around the world, one person at a time. I did not start EHAP so I could be famous or wealthy. But I know that if I am giving my best, life will reward me with the opportunity to touch more lives through television and various media outlets. My perspective is being on Oprah is a tremendous venue to touch lives. When the time is right, the opportunity will appear. When the opportunity presents itself I'll be prepared!

Once I am on Oprah, life as I know it will change because of the number of people who watch her show. Many people have spoken some powerful visions into my life. One friend had a dream I had a nationally syndicated column in major newspapers. A complete stranger called me to tell me she dreamed about me traveling all over the world. Audience members, who have never met me before, will pass me a note or whisper in my ear, "Great things are in store for you." They see and feel my vision. It is indeed overwhelming! Each time someone confirms my vision I consider it a reminder that I am on the right track. If I just keep taking it one day at a time and trust the process as each new level of the vision becomes a reality, I'll be prepared for the challenge.

Oprah has often said, luck is preparation meeting opportunity! I am not waiting on luck to get on her show. I am being prepared for much more than guest appearances on talk shows. I have been preparing all of my life to be an international speaker. I have been speaking professionally since I was twelve years old when my seventh grade English teacher signed me up for my first oratorical speech contest. I have had my own television show in college, entitled "It's on you!" I have worked in radio. I have spoken to a crowd as large as ten thousand. It is all a preparation period. No one and I repeat, no one makes it to the top and stays there without paying the price. Part of the price is the educational segment involved in any career. No matter how much talent you have, you must have a working knowledge of the field. Let me give you an example.

When I visited Oprah's show back in the early 90's, I noticed she shook everyone's hand as they exited after the show. She didn't sign autographs and she didn't take pictures. Hmmm, I thought that was weird. It actually seems very trivial in the big picture of life. But ten years later when I entered the speaking industry, the reason became very clear. When I speak to large crowds I can easily spend an hour or more after each event shaking hands, signing books, conversing with audience members, taking pictures or giving hugs. I don't mind one bit! However, there are times when I am trying to catch a plane or have to attend another engagement and I have to manage my time wisely.

One of my prayers has been I want to remain available to the audience and readers as much as possible. So how do you do this as your vision expands? What seems like a small detail can be a major public relations disaster if you don't handle it correctly. So I took notes from Oprah. I ask people to form some type of line so there is order in what is otherwise a very chaotic situation for all of us. I have learned how to sign books or photos while listening to the person speak at the same time. I try to take photographs at the very end of the engagement or book signing. I also have learned to try to schedule at least two hours after each event for what I call "interaction" time. I can't imagine having had crowds of thousands without having learned this lesson first!

If you have a vision you will need to go through the educational process. You watch other people; you experiment to find out what works and what doesn't. You examine how you feel when someone puts you on hold, brushes you off, or doesn't respond. Compare that to how you feel when a real person answers the phone, sends you a hand written note, or gives you a hug. I have used my interactions with famous people to educate myself on the business. I am a firm believer you must be prepared for success. If you arrive too early you can lose it all because you don't know how to manage it. If you arrive too late, you miss the opportunity. You must pay attention to the timing.

I can honestly say I would not have been ready for Oprah when I wrote the first book. I would not have been prepared for a whirlwind tour of the country. I stumbled through the first two years of business, trying to figure out what I was doing. I struggled in the airports and hotels because I packed too much stuff. I overestimated my product sales and underpriced my presentations. If I struck it rich instantly, I would have probably mismanaged my profits. I struggled to balance my checkbook in the beginning. I spent every dime I made. I didn't know how to budget over the course of a year for a profession, which has various peak seasons. In fact, I know I would have taken some of the success for granted. There were many things I had no interest in learning or dealing with. If I could have paid someone to do certain things I would have. But, they were things I needed to experience. They were experiences, which held valuable lessons. The "process" has really taught me more than I ever learned in seven years of college. Life experience *really* is the best experience. Or as they say in the business world, there is nothing better than on-the-job-training!

I pause here to reflect on the original vision. Remember I told you I saw myself speaking to thousands and thousands of people? Remember I told you there were books selling at a tremendous rate in the back of the convention hall? Remember I told you there were numerous people working for me? Most importantly remember I told you the vision was so huge I was brought to tears. I was overwhelmed and scared at the same time. In the first few years I was growing into my vision. I was developing skills to manage the vision and balance all that comes with such a great calling. I was learning how to control my own emotions and deal with the struggles that accompany "success." As the Bible says, "don't despise the days of small beginnings."

Every success story starts with an ordinary person being trained to do extraordinary things.

I've watched people in the public eye very closely. I've learned one very important lesson, the question shouldn't be when are you going to be on Oprah? The question should be: "when Oprah calls, will you be ready?" I am using this time to prepare myself physically and intellectually in addition to spiritually for the opportunities that I am confident will come, when I am ready! As a person of faith, I am trusting my Creator implicitly with my life. I don't believe the ultimate goal is to be on Oprah or the bestseller lists. Those things would be nice, but they only provide a venue to share my message of hope and strength to individuals who are struggling for personal fulfillment. My focus is on making a difference in everything I do. If I make a difference for one person in an audience of two hundred, mission accomplished!!!

There have been times when only six people showed up for a seminar, three of those were my friends. I have lost money trying to figure out what works and offer quality presentations. You can't focus on what you are losing, you have to focus on the possibilities and what you are learning from the experience. I conducted an empowerment seminar for young ladies, which was well attended, but was short on financial sponsorship. When all was said and done, I owed nine thousand dollars for a twenty thousand dollar event. My initial response was a sense of panic. How was I going to get the money to pay this debt? Why was I ending up in the negative for trying to do something good for young ladies? I had to adjust my attitude after receiving the evaluations from the young ladies. I did not lose nine thousand dollars. I invested it into the lives of the individuals who attended. That was one of the best investments I could make. Investing in people will always pay off!

When only six people show up I give them my best as if I was speaking to a thousand. Professionalism and integrity don't start when you make it. You start the process from day one. You improve with time. No matter what size the audience, I am focusing on using my gift to bless as many people as possible.

So I thank each one of you who believe in my abilities. I thank each one of you for planting seeds of "possibilities!" I thank each one of you for seeing the vision and encouraging me not to settle. I need you to keep pushing, keep believing, keep praying and keep preparing me. And while you are doing that for my vision, I will keep speaking, writing, training and consulting to inspire and empower you to make your vision a reality.

O.K., back to the original question? When am I going to be on Oprah? When I have been prepared for all that will come with appearing on her show. I can promise you, Oprah will be the start of a whole different level of success. Maybe we should be asking this question: "When will Veraunda's show be on the air? And when will Oprah give me the honor of being a guest on my show?" Don't laugh too hard ...it is a definite possibility!

Apply the lesson in this chapter to your life:

Who do you know that has done what you are trying to do?
Now start your research, read about them and learn about their journey.

How will you use your success to help others?

The Closing Argument
"What are you waiting for?"

What are you waiting for? Enough money? The right time? The support of your significant other, spouse, friends or family? For your kids to finish school? There is no such thing as everything being where you want it, when you want it, so there is no better time to make your vision a reality than right now!

You don't have to settle! You have the power to make your dream a reality! When I speak to faith-based organizations, I often share with the audience I am not impressed by the act of Peter stepping out of the boat on the water. Yes, I think it took great faith to believe he would be able to do what seemed impossible. But I believe the miracle in the story is when Peter took his eyes off Jesus as the waters began to stir and the wind was blowing, Jesus did not allow him to drown!

When your storm hits, you must know that no matter what the circumstances, you only fail if you give up on your dream. Don't panic, you are not going to drown! You may have to try different methods. You may have to start more than once. You may have to change business partners, but you can't give up! I have had numerous occasions when I FELT like I was going to drown. But the one thing I held onto as my floating device was the vision. I would say to myself several times a day, "My Creator did not ask me to step out of the boat to let me drown!"

I live by faith now. Learning how to live by faith and trust God on a daily basis has been an incredible experience! Why? Because despite the rough waters, the blowing wind, and the forceful rains in my life, He has NEVER allowed me to drown! I am still here! I am doing what

I was designed to do! I am living my dream! Even on my most challenging days, I realize I am extremely blessed. I am further than I would have predicted for my own life. The vision is becoming a reality one day at a time.

For my first book, *Everything Has A Price!* my publishing consultant came up with the concept of me and a price tag with money falling into my path. I thought, oh yea, that is cool! The photo shoot was fun! When the proofs came back, I said wow! It is amazing what creative people can do with an idea! The graphic artist, photographer, makeup artist and my consultant had produced a winner! I wish I could say I saw their vision for the cover, but to be honest, I just thought it was a cool idea. I never wanted to be on the cover of my book. They saw the vision, I trusted their judgment and the results were a winner!

Now when I look at the cover I see the profoundness of it. I am happy on the cover. Everyone in the room had a really good time in the photo shoot. We had music playing in the background; everyone on the set was jovial. I felt like I was on top of the world. Here's what most people don't know. I had to scrounge up the money to pay the photographer and the make up artist. There were five people present for the photo shoot. We each had to go into our pockets to find money so we could create the illusion of money falling. I think we had about forty dollars between the five of us. My consultant started laughing as we tried to make a few dollars seem like it was falling from the sky. I remember his words very clearly, "Baby, our day is coming! We are going to look back on this day and laugh. I'm so glad that trouble doesn't last always! Oprah, watch out!"

It is awesome to think we shot the cover in an old warehouse with a group of people who were all trying to make their dream a reality. All of us where financially stressed. We shot the photos on the third floor of the building. There was no elevator, so we had to hike up three flights of stairs with clothes, make up and cameras. There was no elaborate set up. So how could I smile the way I did for the photos? Simply put, I loved every minute of the process. The message as I now understand it is that money comes to me as a result of doing what I love. You will have to be patient in addition to having unwavering faith in the process.

Flip back to the cover of this book. What do you see? At twenty-three stories high, the Orange County Courthouse is the tallest building in downtown Orlando. On the right side of the courthouse, the five story building is the State Attorney's Office. I worked on various floors of the building during my tenure as a prosecutor, but the fifth floor was the administrative floor. To get to the top of my profession as a lawyer I would have to become the State Attorney which is an elected position in Florida. The twenty-third floor of the courthouse holds a special courtroom for our big media trials in addition to the office of our Chief Judge. To get to the top of the courthouse I would have to become a judge which at this stage of my life is not my calling. So where did that leave me in terms of my possibilities? I had to make a tough decision about my gift of speaking, my love of people and my desire to make a difference! I was using all of these in the courtroom. However, there is an entire world out here which richly rewards people in overwhelming ways if they find creative ways to use their gifts. My decision was to experiment with my possibilities. There was the potential for me to become an international speaker and author. I decided to pursue that potential!

At first glance the picture appears to be just a scenic background. But if you look closer I am making a strong statement. I have on jeans with my business jacket and a briefcase, which would never be permitted in court! I am also outside of the building, which symbolizes sometimes you have to step out of the box. In my case, it meant walking away from an awesome profession to pursue another possibility. The courthouse and the surrounding complex was my comfort zone. Four years later, I can truthfully say I miss practicing law. However, the freedom I have experienced, the lessons I have learned and the success I have had pursuing my vision has been awesome!

I am living my dream every day I wake up! The journey has been very rocky. I'll be honest, there are days when I have to say a *special* prayer for strength in addition to giving myself a pep talk about the circumstances. I have spent a nice amount of money to promote an independent seminar. I was confident the seminar would be a sellout. When the registrations didn't come in or I walked in the door believing for on-site sellouts which didn't materialize, I have been disappointed. The bonus in doing what you love is even when you are disappointed you love what you are doing so much that you look beyond the moment. I have always spoken like I was one of the best in the world. I simply don't believe in "bad" performances.

I've lost money when I couldn't afford to loose a dime. I've stressed and struggled with the bill collectors. I've had to pay to ship books back to Orlando because the audience didn't buy them. I've temped when I didn't feel like it. I've lost friends along the way. I've cried and I have even lost my temper when things weren't going my way. I have felt like giving up and just going back to what I know is comfortable and safe. During these times my best friend Jaydee would be there by my side, saying, "Don't stress over it. It's going to be just fine." Many other people around the country continue to support me as I travel this journey. My angels show up when I need them the most. So will yours!

Flip back to the cover of this book one more time. Does it look like it poured down rain before we shot the photo? Do you see one dark cloud in the sky? Can you tell the humidity was so high that my hairstylist said, "Veraunda, what about a straight look?" No, you can't! It looks like it was a gorgeous day in Central Florida. But looks can be deceiving.

There was no rain in the forecast for our morning photo shoot. Imagine my surprise when I arrived at nine in the morning to start the hair and make up session and there was a light drizzle. My photographer, Rafael turned to the weather channel to double check our forecast. According to the meteorologist, there was not going to be rain until later in the evening. There was one problem, it was pouring down now! The sky was a dark gray. It didn't look like it was going to stop anytime soon. The fear factor tried to start talking to me:

Keisha: Girl, what are you going to do now? You have set this timeline to complete the book and I don't think we are going to make it. The situation doesn't look good. Rafael travels all around the country. You probably won't be able to get back on his calendar for at least a month. That will be too late for your deadline. Oooh, this is a disaster! The whole day is going to be wasted.

I wanted to scream, "Houston, we have a problem here! It is raining right now! Why isn't one of your radars picking this up?" Instead, I refocused my energy. Rafael told Elsie to start on my make up. He was sure the rain was only temporary. He was right. By the time Elsie finished my hair and make up, the sun was trying to peak through the clouds. There was still a light drizzle. Rafael told us to get in the car. He believed by the time we reached the courthouse the drizzle would stop, he could see the sun pushing the clouds out of the way. I said a quick prayer, "Lord, you didn't bring me this far to leave me!" Rafael was absolutely right! The rain was only temporary! The sun prevailed over the clouds. We got great photos! Our patience combined with proceeding to prepare paid off!

Would you believe as soon as we left the courthouse, the rain started pouring down again? Ha, Ha, Ha! It didn't matter now, because we had captured our vision on film! What I needed...I had! The photo is an awesome reminder, sometimes you just need to weather the storm. Sooner or later, it will pass!

Living your dream is not going to be easy. Life isn't fair! People will really disappoint you. People will hurt you along the way. Some will be intentional others will be unintentional. Regardless of their motives it is painful. There will be people waiting for you to fail. I believe those people will be extremely disappointed because failure is not an option! Think of our challenges as experimenting with our possibilities. The more we work at it, the more we pursue our visions, the more they will see our Creator's hands at work. He is refining us, preparing us and promoting us!

Remember to just embrace the vision at the very moment you feel like quitting, the provision will show up. 2002 was a very challenging year for me. I was trying to write this book when my mother died unexpectedly of cancer. I tried working for an entity, which I believed, would solve all my financial problems and allow me the freedom to cultivate my company. It didn't work out. I decided to start looking for a job to sustain me. Several things crossed my path that looked wonderful and very promising. I spoke with my accountant at length discussing the possibilities. We decided if I went back to work for a governmental agency, I could eliminate my credit debt in two years. We looked at the profit from EHAP. I had met my yearly goal but couldn't figure out why I was still struggling. My accountant reinforced the need for me to stay focused. "Veraunda, you are on the right track. Don't get distracted and give up on EHAP Inc. It's just a matter of time."

I tried to design my own path. I applied for several jobs I thought would make my life better. I would get excited about the possibility of the "full-time" position. I would map out the financial relief the "job" could provide. The door of opportunity seemed wide open! In the back of my head I would always hear this little voice saying, "Veraunda, you are not living in your truth!"

Lucy: Veraunda, you have been clear about your vision from day one. Be very careful about running back to a "comfortable place."

Keisha: Girl, the vision is clear, the path is unknown, so it isn't going to matter what you do, in the meantime. You have to take care of yourself! It is completely OK to make ends meet until the vision provides you with the means to support it. And Lucy, for the record, I am not being negative!

Lucy: It is easy to get sucked back into the box. I'm not telling you not to go back to work for a entity that will help you on the journey, but I am telling you to make sure that whatever you do, it will enhance your journey, not halt your journey or change your direction.

Keisha: Well, it is about time! Lucy is finally getting it! We have to do what we have to do!

Lucy: No, Keisha, I am not settling. We have to walk by faith, pursue our dreams, and make wise decisions every step of the way. Keisha, you are desperate. I on the other hand have a strong confidence in our Creator's promises to make sure we are never forsaken if we stay focused and faithful.

The process is amazing because if you trust the process you can't lose. I had to learn delayed doesn't mean denied, it means next! Next opportunity. Next level. Next relationship. There was a period of two years when it felt like I was losing big time. I lost my mother.

I didn't get my "job." I lost a best friend. Actually, I lost a couple of friends. I applied for four wonderful jobs based on referrals from colleagues or friends. I would make it to the final selection process each time. The doors of opportunity seemed to close each time.

Lucy: *Live in your truths! Don't you dare let these jobs fool you! You didn't want to work an 8-5 job. You didn't want to wear a suit everyday. You are enjoying your freedom, your flexibility. There is a place for you, but it will be a place that allows you to fulfill your divine purpose. You are called to greatness! You know it deep inside of you. Stay focused! One day at a time! One step at time! Just enjoy the ride...the entire ride! Your day is coming soon. Don't mistake these temporary situations as a reflection of your future. You are doing very well despite all of the obstacles. You are still one of the best-kept secrets in the world! You are changing lives around this country. You, Veraunda, do not have to settle!*

As you are reading this you might be thinking, Veraunda I have really enjoyed your stories, BUT, I need a formula. How do I make my vision a reality? Where do I start? How am I going to finance this dream? The questions are forming like a whirlwind in your mind. Stop them! Just quiet them at this very moment! Get still in your spirit. Now ask yourself this question: "What do I really have to lose, if I don't try?" Now counter that question with asking yourself, "What if I make it?"

It's that simple. You have to start with looking at the possibilities! Once you become excited about the possibilities, you come up with a plan. Don't make this a complicated process or you will let fear sneak back in and overtake the vision. The plan for my company was very simple: First I went to the bookstore and found books on publishing and speaking. Next, I started developing the tools they suggested. I tried them out one at a time, and when they didn't work out, I tried something else. I journaled the entire process, so I would always have a reference point of what my goal was, and how far I had come. For example when I started speaking I charged $250.00 per hour. My written plan was to raise that fee each year. I set a date to leave my job, and stuck with it, despite the fears that grew as the date inched closer. Finally, I made up my mind that failure was not an option for me!

Summary:
1) Research your vision to figure out what it will take to make it a reality.
2) Develop a plan, then be ready to readjust the plan.
3) Be willing to do the work...all of it! (Even when you don't feel like it!)
4) Work your plan like your life depends on it...because it does!

Even when I felt like life was completely out of control, life provided constant encouragement and reminders, I couldn't quit. One of my most profound experiences occurred at the beginning of 2003 as I was finishing this book. I decided to place a call to Les Brown to wish him a happy New Year on Monday, the 4th of January. He was busy when I called but asked me what I had on my schedule later in the evening. He had someone he wanted me to meet. I reported I would be free once I finished teaching around five. We made tentative plans to talk after my class. Les called me back with an invitation to dinner. He never told me who he wanted me to meet or why he wanted me to meet this person.

I arrived at the restaurant with no idea of what the evening would hold. I was pleasantly surprised to see two handsome young men at a private table near the back of the restaurant. One was Les; the other I soon found out was a billionaire! He was probably in his late 30's or early 40's. We all chatted over dinner making the normal general exchanges about who we were, what we did, etc. Needless to say I was the least accomplished at the table. However, I was excited to be there. The voices were talking:

Lucy: Girl, look at this! Here you are sitting with a millionaire and a billionaire! God is awesome.

Keisha: Yep, you are sitting here with two rich men and you are on the verge of not being able to pay for your own dinner. This is nice, but are they going to pay for your dinner or better yet invest in your company?

Lucy: Keisha, You don't get it do you? This is about the possibilities! Veraunda, this dinner is not about how much money you don't have at this moment, it is about showing you what's possible through two people who have made it by living their dreams. It's what you are writing the book about remember?

The dinner guest had been on the verge of bankruptcy several years before when he made up his mind he was going to make a million dollars. He didn't have a college degree but was passionate about network marketing and training. He had a vision of how he could help companies make mega money. That vision made him one million dollars each year for five years. In 2002, his company made him a billionaire.

I sat there listening to his story in awe. Here I was finishing a book about not settling and realizing your possibilities when a billionaire shows up to confirm the entire premise of my book. It gets deeper! As we were finishing dinner, the billionaire asked me what was next for me. I said I honestly didn't know. I explained I just wanted to be a blessing. He asked me in what way did I want to bless people. He instructed me to be specific. This was a hard question because at that moment it wasn't a reality. But, I responded by saying I want to be wealthy enough to pay off people's bills, provide scholarships and live a comfortable life. I followed that sentence by saying I was certain of a few things. I shared my vision of speaking to millions of people around the world. I told him I was positive I would be wealthy some day. In the meantime, I was trying to enjoy and trust the process. This journey could be overwhelming on some days. I was accustomed to working for the government or other people. I was comfortable doing my job, getting a paycheck direct deposited and having insurance. I was way out of my element now. It was very difficult at times to focus on what was next. What I did know is when I spoke, people were inspired. People were telling me they felt empowered. I would get letters, emails and phone calls affirming that individuals were making positive changes in their lives after reading my book or hearing me speak. I was making a difference!

The billionaire listened intently, then asked me how much I charged. I told him I constantly battled with my fees. I took pride in being affordable and found it hard to say no to people. I concluded by saying my non-profit rate for an hour was much more than I made as an attorney working a full day, so I found pricing the most difficult part of my business. I often wish I had someone to deal with the business while I just showed up to speak. The billionaire looked me directly in the eye, then blew me away with these words:

"Veraunda, you deserve it! Whatever "it" is...you deserve it! All of it!"

There was no lecture, no explanation. The words were so powerful, I felt my heart beating in my chest. How did he know? Where did those words come from? It was a very different way to say, "You don't have to settle." I hadn't breathed a word about this book or the title. I hadn't breathed a word about looking for a job. Yet, his spirit picked up on my dilemma of settling in my own life.

Les chimed in; "I've tried to get her to leave the chitlin circuit. I've listened to her tape, she is very talented! She is powerful and passionate! But she doesn't want to leave." I'm sure I sounded like an eight-year-old when I said, "Les, that's not true! I..." The billionaire stopped me mid sentence: "If it's not true then what are you waiting for? Remember, you deserve IT Veraunda...all of IT!"

My closing argument for you to consider today is simply:

You can't afford to wait another year, month or day to start living your dream! You don't have to settle! You can do what you love and make money doing it! If you have a vision, it is calling you to your destiny. The only thing stopping you from living your dream is YOU. Specifically, it is the voice of fear and worry telling you to think about the mountain of "what ifs." It is a little nagging voice telling you to stay where you are because you are safe there. It's telling you it's better to be unhappy than kicked out of your house or finding another job. The voice is telling you this is the best you can do. It's not so bad. It's telling you if you just wait, sometime in the future, your life will be different and you'll be able to do it later. It's telling you right now it's stormy out there, you'll drown if you leave this comfortable boat.

I am telling you to listen to the other voice. The voice of your vision! It's telling you if you think about your current situation, you may be drowning, despite being in the boat. The boat you are in, is already being tossed and turned in the storms of life. You can drown despite being in the boat. If the storm tips the boat over, then what are you going to do? My suggestion is jump out there and remember you have already been prepared for this very moment. Life has been teaching you how to swim since the day you were born. Now it is just a test of your faith and endurance! Angels will always appear when you need them! The voice of the vision and the unexpected angels will guide you in the right direction. When a door closes, it is for a reason! When you stray off the path, you will know it! Just be still for a moment, get your thoughts together, refocus and get back on track.

When the finances seem to choke everything out of you, remember it is only temporary. Don't give up! Get creative. Financial storms are one of the toughest challenges you will face. We all need a place to live, electricity, transportation, food and clothing. When these items are threatened in any way the pressure feels insurmountable. You must believe with everything in you it is only temporary. This too shall pass!

I started saving one dollar a day at one of the most difficult times in my finances. I made a decision I would not allow the appearance of my finances to control my thought process. I continued to tithe to my church. I forced myself to give an offering. I decided to detach myself from materialism. My attitude became, if I sow into the lives of others I will reap what I sow. I gave away furniture to people who really needed it without having a way to replace it. I cleaned out my closet to donate to charity. I began to realize as long as I invest in the lives of others, I could never experience a state of lack.

You must do the same thing. Sow into the lives of others when it hurts. It sounds crazy, but try it. Try to find ways to bless others in your darkest financial hour. I have done this on many occasions. The results are amazing. I have always had gas in my car. The tank has been on empty, yet I made it from point A to B. I haven't always been able to eat what I wanted, but I have never missed a meal. I have had to extend my bill due date, but my lights have never been turned off. I choose to bless when I feel myself struggling with finances. I remind myself, even on my worst day, I am blessed. I see the miracles in my life everyday. Everything I need I have at this moment. I have learned the power of living in the present moment. If you master this, your life will change tremendously.

You will eliminate the needless worry about things you don't have control over. Work hard, learn from your mistakes, read books and do research about your finances, then watch your wealth materialize as you pursue your dream.

Don't get distracted by those people who don't care because they don't have a vision of their own or are jealous of your vision. Remember, misery loves company! Become determined to dwell in the presence of your enemies knowing that a table is being prepared for you. Many of your enemies will end up being servants having taught you valuable lessons in the process of your journey. Remember, everyone will not travel the entire distance with you. Know when to walk away and embrace the positive lessons you have learned while they were traveling with you. Don't get stuck in the goodbye. Don't stop to mourn the loss for a long period of time. You must keep moving. Rest for a moment if you need to, but get back up, refocus and get back on track. Instead, figure out who cares. For every person that drops by the wayside, there will be another person who will pick up where they left off. The baton will be passed to another individual who is capable and qualified to run the next leg of the race with you. Who cares about your vision? Who cares about your well-being? Who has proven to be supportive when you needed them? Who is cheering for you? Who can you hear telling you not to give up? Who is saying come on, you can do it? Embrace those who sincerely care about you and eliminate the ones who don't.

Focus on the calm voice whispering in your ear. What is it telling you? Do you want to go back to college? Do you want to move up in the company? Do you want to change careers? Do you want to start your own company? Do you want to pay off your debt? Do you have a desire to travel? What's your dream? What have you been preparing for? What are you exceptionally good at? What would you be happiest doing? What do you love so much you that would you do it for free? If you listen closely I bet it is your own version of Lucy with the bottom line and the last word:

Lucy: "You don't have to settle, your vision can become a reality...after all, you deserve it...ALL OF IT!" What are you waiting for?

VERAUNDA I. JACKSON

Veraunda conducts professional or personal development
workshops for companies, universities,
and various organizations in addition to
presenting keynote addresses.

For more information please contact her at:
Veraunda I. Jackson, Esquire
EHAP Inc.
P.O. Box 1150
Orlando, Florida 32802
407-445-1766 phone
407-445-0266 fax
or
send your inquiry via e-mail to:
ehapinc@aol.com

Visit Veraunda's website:
www.ehapinc.com

BOOK & TAPE
ORDER FORM

EHAP Inc.
Everything Has A Price!
P.O. Box 1150
Orlando, Florida 32802

407-445-1766 (p) or 407-445-0266 (f)
• Visit my website, www.ehapinc.com to order.
• Credit Card orders - fax or mail this order form
  for an autographed copy.

Name:_____

Address:_____

City, State, Zip:_____

Phone:_____

Name for Autograph:_____

Book: You Don't Have To Settle ____ x $18.00*= $ _____

Book: Everything Has A Price ____ x $18.00*= $ _____

Tape: Everything Has A Price ____ x $12.00*= $ _____

Tape: Legally Structuring Your Business ____ x $12.00*= $ _____

TOTAL = $ _____
*Includes shipping and handling

_____ I have enclosed a check or money order

_____ I am ordering by credit card

Credit Card Type *(Circle)*:   VISA   MC

Number _____

Exp Date:_____ Total authorized: $_____

Signature_____

YOU DON'T HAVE TO SETTLE!